Other Books by Mortimer Levitt:

How to Start Your Own Business

Without Losing Your Shirt 1988

Class: What It Is and How to Acquire It 1984

The Executive Look: How to Get It —How to Keep It 1981

The Executive Look Seminars 1979

NINETY SIX

AND TOO BUSY TO DIE

A LIFE BEYOND THE AGE OF DYING

BY
MORTIMER LEVITT

About Aspatore Books – Publishers of C-Level Business Intelligence
Aspatore Books (www.Aspatore.com) is the largest and most exclusive publisher of C-Level executives (CEO, CFO, CTO, CMO, Partner) from the world's most respected companies. Aspatore annually publishes a select group of C-Level executives from the Global 1,000, top 250 professional services firms, law firms (Partners & Chairs), and other leading companies of all sizes. C-Level Business Intelligence ™, as conceptualized and developed by Aspatore Books, provides professionals of all levels with proven business intelligence from industry insiders – direct and unfiltered insight from those who know it best – as opposed to third-party accounts offered by unknown authors and analysts. Aspatore Books is committed to publishing a highly innovative line of business books, and redefining such resources as indispensable tools for all professionals.

ACKNOWLEDGMENTS

Behind every good man there is good support. In this instance, I want to acknowledge the help I received from Pamela Aguilar and Dr. Peter Slater

* * * * *

The names used in Mr. Levitt's sexual ventures are all fictitious.

For Mimi,

Without whom I wouldn't be.

Mimi and Mortimer on the street where they live.

"I know I must die but I'm beginning to think they're making me an exception"

William Saroyan

"Success in business is not for the greedy – on the contrary, success results from giving more, without charging more and the possibilities are infinite."

Mortimer Levitt

Contents

INTRODUCTION   10

436 FRANKLIN AVENUE: THE BEGINNING   16

ADOLESCENCE: I BECOME A CIRCUS BAREBACK RIDER   25

IN 1923, I BEGIN A "NON-CAREER   31

MY FIRST WIFE: THE GLAMOROUS ANNA FLEISHER FRIEDE   43

I OPEN MY FIRST CUSTOM SHOP   52

ELEMENTS OF MY ASTONISHING SUCCESS   62

OUR TRICKY DIVORCE   71

IN 1941, THREE YEARS AND TEN MONTHS FROM THE BEGINNING, I RETIRE   75

IN 1942, I OPEN THE MORTIMER LEVITT GALLERY   85

THE HIGH LIFE   90

I MEET MIMI AND MY REAL LIFE BEGINS   104

MARRIED LIFE: AFTER THE HONEYMOON   118

MORTIMER'S RESTAURANT - GLENN BERNBAUM   129

REAL ESTATE: MY SECRET BONANZA   133

HEROIN: SYNANON AND DAYTOP VILLAGE   136

UP TO OUR NECKS IN CULTURE   141

THE LEVITT PAVILION FOR THE PERFORMING ARTS   156

1991, FIFTY YEARS LATER, I'M BACK AT CUSTOM SHOP   166

NINETY-SIX AND TOO BUSY TO DIE   174

OLD AGE AND EVEN HAPPIERS? YES!   181

KEEP SMILING   186

EPILOGUE   197

Introduction

They kept telling me to write another book. At the very least, perhaps, a memoir about my ridiculously uneven life that started at the very bottom, and then bumped along a path that ended with a diversity of successful activities: unexpected success in business, in the arts and music, in education, and in advancing the treatment of heroin addicts, as well as in a plethora of other things. However, most autobiographies, at least the forty-one that I have read, have all had dreadful downsides, really dark stuff: sex abuse, mental breakdowns, drug and alcohol addiction, incest, betrayal, and unexpected violence. As I am fortunate enough to have no such dark side, I thought there would be only minimal interest my memoir.

Then, one day, I realized, quite out of the blue, that I am well into my nineties and despite what I had been led to believe about the frightfulness of aging, my life is far more enjoyable than it has ever been. Here I am, living long past the age of dying, busy, busy, busy, and still looking ahead. Frankly, I really am too busy to die. My extended life is an undeserved bonus that may make for an engaging read – certainly more so than the now "commonplace" of incest, addiction, depression, and you may add, the endless list of troubles that have plagued the lives of so many other writers.

I certainly am not a conventional businessman nor a conventional anything for that matter, and the older I become, the more I realize how completely different I am from friends. I do not watch sports on television although I have been an avid tennis player, an avid skier, and a relentless sailor. I have strong political beliefs but prefer to express them in writing rather than in fruitless discourse. I have no interest in bridge, gin rummy, chess, or computer games. Furthermore, I seem to have always been controversial.

Introduction

To sum up, I decided to write this book to detail a long, long life from the perspective of a high school flunk-out. My story is in its way, inspirational: the story of a lifetime *in reverse*. In my ninety-sixth year, I am happier than I was in my thirty-fourth year, the year I retired from the day-to-day management of my business, although I continued to be the sole owner of eighty-two Custom Shops for sixty years. Now that's a long time. On two occasions, employees opened competing businesses that died in puberty, and there has not been a single chain to compete successfully – not one. For sixty-years, I have been one-of-a-kind, a record of some kind in this highly competitive country. To some, this might sound like a broken record, the American rags-to-riches fable: it isn't!

Because I had flunked almost every subject in high school, I concluded that I was not smart. My low high school grades were in line with my being a slow reader. In 1942 New York University had a program to correct reading problems. That course did not increase the speed of my reading, but it led to one very important conversation. The professor who headed the program called me into her office and said, "Mr. Levitt, we do not usually reveal the results of our IQ tests," (I didn't know I had taken one), "but at your age (thirty-five), you should know that you have a high IQ (142). So that is <u>not</u> why you are a slow reader." I said, "What is the significance of 142?" She said, "Mr. Levitt, the average IQ is 100; 160 is genius. Mr. Levitt you are smart enough to recognize the value of a 142 IQ. You **are** a slow reader, but you're smart. Congratulations." My secretary checked back with Boy's High School, and the score there was 141. After all those many years, that kind woman made an important change in the way I saw myself. My success was evidently no fluke.

Some thirty-five years ago, the publisher of *Who's Who in America* invited members to submit an original quotation relating to their philosophy. My quote was one of those accepted: "Success in business is not for the greedy. On the contrary, success results from giving more without charging more, and the possibilities are infinite."

I had become addicted to short stories, those in *The New Yorker*, a breed apart: E.B White, Irwin Shaw, Robert Coates, Brendan Gill, John O'Hara, William Maxwell, Lillian Ross, and all the others –I read them all, I loved them. To me, their stories were a "wonderment," I was in total awe! Yet, one day, back in 1941,

I took a deep breath and thought to myself, "I will try to write a short story." I was single, there was no one around to see my failure. I had never written anything other than copy for Custom Shop windows; nevertheless I would try.

To acquire the basics, I took a course in elementary grammar at New York University's Adult Education Division. There I learned only one thing of value: the name of an eighty-five-page book, *The Elements of Style* by Strunk and White. That well-renowned little book opened my eyes to the true craft of writing. My last three books were published by Atheneum, one of our more prestigious publishers. Most important, there have been no ghostwriters ever. I have written every word, including these.

In 1947, Irwin Shaw was holding a master class at New York University; Shaw (*The Young Lions*) was my hero. I had no qualifications, but persuaded him to accept me. In the first session, Shaw asked me to read my best story to the class. I finished reading *Big Shot,* and took my seat. Shaw said, "Surely Mr. Levitt can't be serious." Not one word about the story, nothing about content or style, nothing. It was devastating, but that is not the end of the story.

Exactly forty years later in 1987, my wife, Mimi and I were guests of Rita and Herbert Salzman at their chalet in Klosters, Switzerland, Shaw's hometown. Mimi was an ardent skier who skied for fifty-seven years (I skied for fifty-five years). Herbert and Rita gave a cocktail party so we could meet some of their local friends, one of whom was Irwin Shaw, forty years older and forty pounds heavier. Later that week, Mimi and I hosted a dinner party. Shaw was one of our guests and on the following day, I lunched with him at his place. I reminded him of that heartless dismissal of my short story. He had no recollection; after all, forty years had passed. "Mortimer, if you still have the story, send it, but only if it has not been edited." I said, "The paper is turning brown at the edges." I mailed the story from New York. Six weeks later he returned it. He had scribbled on the front page, "Mortimer, I haven't changed my mind."

Of course, being ninety-six meant a few things had to change. I gave up downhill skiing at eighty-five, playing tennis (singles only) when I was eighty-six, and stopped sailing my boat alone at eighty-seven. I have lost most of my ability to play the piano because my fingers have lost their former authority. My left hand shakes, and that's not all. Like you, I forget names; but you forget them at retail and I forget them at wholesale. I still drive comfortably during the day but at night I have to be very, very careful.

Recently, when after a pleasant visit with my dermatologist, I reached the building lobby, I realized I had forgotten my umbrella. I went back to get it and, as I approached the street door for a second time, the head nurse came running out with my attaché case, apparently forgotten when I went back for the umbrella.

So how does one live with that kind of nuisance? Quite simply, with my personal philosophy: "A variety of endless troubles is indeed the price we all must pay for the gift of life; there are no exceptions – there are NO exceptions." The first "no exception" is for me, and the second "no exception" is for you, whoever you are. But don't despair; as compensation, you have been blessed with orgasms sweetened with the fleeting moments of love. To sum it up, life is a crapshoot.

This insight has spared me considerable anguish. When serious trouble hits, don't cast your eyes to heaven and mumble, "Dear God, why me?" If God deems to answer, the answer would be, "Why not you?" Remember this: life is a crapshoot, and there is no reward for good behavior or punishment for bad behavior (other than a guilty conscience). Above all, and no matter what, don't feel sorry for yourself.

Without a downside, there could be no upside. I have listed some of the downsides of aging but the upside not only compensates, it adds a plus. I enjoy being with people and I thoroughly enjoy being Mimi's husband. I'm comfortable with people always, at all times, and in all places. This came only with aging. At theater I talk to people to the right of me and people to the left. After the show, I am apt to ask of anyone next to me, "Tell me, would you recommend this show to a friend?" I am "comfortable in my own skin" and comfortable with making decisions.

Overall, there is the thrill of having lived through so many learning experiences. I dance as well as I did when I was younger, my sense of rhythm being unaffected. Obviously, I don't have the staying power but if I really like the beat, I go all out, taking a break after about five minutes. Don't be greedy, you cannot have everything.

John McEnroe was born with an aptitude for tennis; Mozart was born with an aptitude for composing; I was born (don't laugh) with an aptitude for enhancing image. I was really gifted. In 1941, just three years and ten months from the day I started my business, *Custom Shop Shirtmakers*, I retired from the day-to-day management. I did not want to be a businessman.

Having given up the day-to-day management of my business, I had the time and interest for other activities. I became a founder of The Manhattan Theater Club where I produced and presented some twenty-two plays in my "Chamber Theater" series. For the past twenty-eight years, I have been an active board member of Lincoln Center's Film Society (New York's Annual Film Festival), and I also hold a record-breaking term of almost thirty years as chairman of Young Concert Artists. I opened The Mortimer Levitt Gallery (1943-1955), at 16 West Fifty-Seventh Street, and founded the Levitt Pavilion for the Performing Arts in Westport, Connecticut. The Levitt Pavilion, a beautifully landscaped amphitheater now in its thirtieth year, offers fifty-five nights of magic, the magic of music under the stars with no admission charge ever.

Back in 1942, my psychoanalyst, Dr. Leonard Blumgart, said, "Mortimer, you have a unique aptitude. You can pick up the mere wisp of a fact and see directly into the core of a problem. And you then usually come up with a simple solution. This is in contrast with other executives who assemble all the facts and then fail to arrive at a desirable interpretation." I was skeptical. After all, Dr. Blumgart was getting paid to make me feel good. Yet, many years later, I realized he had been quite serious, that I actually do have an aptitude for simplifying. To my surprise, I have created a mixed bag of suggested solutions for some of our country's chronic problems.

As I review them now these suggestions might indicate a certain arrogance. After all, who am I, with my lack of education and lack of experience in government, to suggest solutions to problems that continue to plague the country? Yet I do believe these concepts can improve, if not cure completely, these plague-like issues. It is my hope that outlining these simple solutions in this book will bring them to the attention of someone whose experience will have qualified him or her to head up one of these projects. When that happens, I can back the effort with financing, as needed.

Getting back to why I am so busy, I am hoping to pay for the construction of new Levitt Pavilions in some twenty cities coast-to-coast, plus paying half the cost of the entertainment. I have created three different educational courses: one for Bard College, one for Mercy College, and one for a group of high schools on Long Island. There is also a concept (a paper, if you will) to stop the growth of juvenile delinquency, and a second paper that can simplify the enormous problems of welfare. It will actually make welfare productive. And finally, there is a freshman course on the value of mnemonics.

I have lived life in my own style and I would like to end it in style. "My Living Will" almost guarantees that I can leave this world smiling, as it includes a request for at least one shot of heroin. I will then enjoy that forbidden pleasure, an experience I cannot risk until I become terminal. You might think of my heroin shot as dessert, my last orgasm. After the heroin, I will be ready to move on to morphine, lots and lots of morphine. I once had an injection in 1933 after a skiing accident, and it was something like divine. I understood how easily one might get hooked.

If you can think of a better way to exit, put it on paper, I'm open to suggestions. As I see it however, *"living through the act of dying is indeed life's ultimate adventure."* (Levitt) And if you think about it, dying is routine. You would be joining up with all the greats: Franklin Roosevelt, Churchill, Hitler, Napoleon, Lawrence Olivier, Marilyn Monroe, Plato, and Einstein –the list is really infinite. If each one of them got through the experience of dying, you can too. For me, it's almost a breeze because there is no eternal life for Jews; most other religions all promise eternal life. Introductions are written to induce browsers to become buyers, so read on. The sex, such as it is, comes later.

1

436 Franklin Avenue:

The Beginning

I was born in 1907 on the twenty-eighth of February, in a four-story brick house at 436 Franklin Avenue in Brooklyn. My parents bought it in partnership with my paternal grandparents, and that's where I grew up, at least for my first twelve years. Unfortunately, I am woefully ignorant of our background. I have no idea how my parents met, what my mother was doing when they met, where she was working, if she was working, what my father did for a living, although they were not blue collar. I do know that my mother was one year old when she arrived here from Berlin and my father was five years old when he arrived from Russia. Mother spoke no German; father spoke no Russian. I can no longer learn anything more because I'm the only one alive except for my kid brother, Ray, who is ninety-three, and knows no more than I. It is hard to understand this lack of curiosity because curiosity is, for me, second nature.

As sex will not play an important role in this memoir, I thought I should dispose of it quickly, get it out of the way.

At ninety-six, need I add, I obviously have a memory problem. Mack Lipkin was our doctor and long-time friend. On my sixty-fifth birthday I saw him for my annual visit, and he said, "Mortimer, from now on you will begin having memory problems. Pay no attention to it, just handle it the best you can. It happens more or less to everyone."

How right he was, with one exception. When it comes to sex, my mind is crystal clear and I remember almost all of the early years, including, surprisingly, the names.

So, let's begin with Aunt Rose. Our extended family shared a four-story brick house in Brooklyn, in an area now known as Bedford-Stuyvesant, a Brooklyn parallel of Harlem. My mother, father, and two younger brothers lived in the first two floors, while my paternal grandparents' family had the top two floors. In one of the two third-floor bedrooms, Aunt Rose and Aunt Gussie shared a double bed. One morning around 5:30 a.m., Aunt Rose woke to discover me, at the age of four, under her nightgown trying to find out how girls were built differently than boys. As there was no punishment for this precocious behavior, I continued on my wayward course. Ruth Bornman, the rosy-cheeked, vivacious daughter of a doctor, a kindergarten classmate, told me how babies are born. Although she was a doctor's daughter and should have known, I refused to believe it.

Our only childhood vacation, two weeks with a farmer's family in the Catskills.
I already look dapper.

When I was seven, our neighbor Mrs. Smith caught me conducting further examination. This time it was Roslyn, her older daughter. Mrs. Smith told Mother, who asked me, "Mortimer, is this true?" I said, "No, Mother." My mother's face went red with rage. She grabbed me by the ear and said, "I'll teach you not to lie. You are not going to forget this." She pulled me over to the sink and said, "Open your mouth," then washed my mouth out with soap. If you have never tasted soap, it is quite unpleasant, and indeed I never forgot it.

However, Mother did not believe that was sufficient punishment, and insisted that father take me to the second floor in the front room, to give me a spanking. She gave him a wooden soup ladle. My father was not up to administering this kind of punishment and I was not ready to take it from him. Although he did give me one whack, the ladle, which was old and worn, broke. As it turned out, we were all happy although I should point out that even at this early age, I had no respect for my father.

As I recall, Sylvia Saphire was next. At age eight, Sylvia was one step up in my adventures, with a totally different approach. You might say I was going in backwards. Her parents owned the candy store on the corner, and we were in the empty store above it. That was a one-time incident, experimental, and never repeated. I was about nine when Ed Cassidy, an alumnus of the Catholic school around the corner, showed several of us younger kids the ritual of masturbation in the vestibule of an untenanted house –not very attractive.

I was a Boy Scout and not a proficient one, I might add. One night after a joint meeting with the Girl Scouts, another boy and I were invited by two girls back to one of their homes. We turned off all the lights, and that was my first experience in "necking." I was permitted to put one hand on a bare breast, another not-to-be-forgotten "moment."

Saphire's candy store was on one corner of our street and the Bornsteins owned the candy store on the other corner. Abe, their son, was four years older and an occasional friend. He was over at our home one night when my parents were out. He made a strong homosexual overture that I rejected out of hand – no pun intended.

I also "had" Pearl Bryant in the bathroom. We were, shall I say, "making out" (not really). There was a bathroom at the end of the third floor hall. My Uncle

Jack heard us talking through the door and whatever he heard was enough. He forced us to open the door and threw us out.

My mother was quite beautiful. I have no picture of my father.

Mother dominated our family. My father was quiet, gentle, and hen-pecked. He was not a breadwinner. Mother held him in deep contempt, though I never knew why. On the first day of kindergarten, Mother gave him the job of taking me to school. When we arrived I began to cry and said I didn't want to go to school. The teachers sent us to the principal's office. I was in complete rebellion. I kicked my father and kicked the principal. The principal said, "You'd better take Mortimer home." The next day, Mother brought me to kindergarten and there was no more nonsense. Her last words were, "Mortimer, sit next to a cleanly dressed girl." I sat between two, Ruth Bornman and Ruth Clayton. Both, as it turned out, were doctors' daughters. Ruth Clayton had long straight hair and a rather soulful expression. Ruth Bornman, in contrast, had a chubby face with red cheeks, blue eyes, and a bright, outgoing personality. She was my favorite.

Sitting next to a cleanly dressed girl nurtured my instincts as a designer. As it turned out, I was from the very beginning a "dresser." Dressing well (with style, not fashion) is the result of an aptitude. Aptitudes are sprinkled here and there by fate or, if you prefer, by the hand of God.

My personal aptitude was a feeling for clothes and that would one day lead to my success in business.

We were three boys, and we all went to P.S. Three on Jefferson Street, two blocks from home. I was the oldest, Ray was three years younger, and Paul was five years younger. We never really became friends. However, when I was ten, the three of us made a frontal attack on Uncle Nathan, the only rich relative in the entire conglomerate. Uncle Nathan was married to Aunt Molly, my father's older sister. Uncle Nathan had a jewelry store on Grand Street, dealing in diamonds and gold jewelry. He also had a Cadillac Limousine and chauffeur. The Hermans lived in an upscale apartment on Quincy Street, Brooklyn's equivalent of New York's Upper East Side. Ray, Paul, and I would walk there around 11:00 on Sunday morning to say hello, and each of us was rewarded with a nickel. Uncle Nathan was a benign gentleman, kind and gracious. His son, Irving, was already a high school senior. I have a faint recollection that each of us was also given a chocolate. That was my first peek into upscale living.

Sunday morning, we dressed up and walked to Uncle Nathan's town house. We each got a nickel.

As it turned out, during World War II, my brother Ray was a photographer in the Navy's Signal Corps and spent most of the war in Washington. Paul was also a photographer in the Signal Corps and as fate would have it, he was killed in Iwo Jima in a most ignominious way. He was riding in a truck when they hit a land mine. What a waste. As head of family, I had a deferment. In addition, my factory was qualified to make officer uniforms, which also lengthened my deferment. Just about the time my deferment ran its course, I turned thirty-seven, too old to be drafted.

My mother and father fought bitterly ever since I can remember, mostly over money, more specifically over the lack of it. Mother had a deep resentment of my father and she absolutely hated his father. I remember one particular occasion when my father was standing in the dining room and my mother at the entrance to the kitchen. They were yelling at each other. I must have been five and was standing alongside my mother when she pressed me to her right hip saying, "This is my flesh and blood," a propos of what I don't know. My reaction was immediate. I knew instantly that I was not my mother's flesh and blood. As a result, I became, and still am, fiercely independent, unable to say "yes" to anyone or anything unless I am in agreement.

I lived with my mother until I was twenty-nine (cultural mores were different back then). I never came home late without phoning; mother always knew where I was. I was never really a loving son although I was a dutiful one. Mother was very, very proud of her "three boys," and they were her life. For me, that was a turnoff. I knew that when I grew up, my life would never be dependent upon the love of children. By my individualized way of thinking, families consisted of people who should be treated as people. If they are likeable, you like them, but you're not obliged to love them. It is probable that I have carried the "I am me" thing too far. Neither was I a loving member of our family - not a black sheep exactly, but rather the off-color dog in a litter.

My parents did not entertain. I did not know about entertaining until the Bryants moved next door. Their children were Pearl, Buster, and Helen. Helen became a missionary, Buster wound up working for the telephone company, and I lost track of Pearl. Mrs. Bryant and Mother became fast friends. Mr. Bryant seldom spoke, and was usually seen comfortably reading in his Morris chair. But the Bryants entertained frequently. I realized that we did not entertain and felt greatly deprived. The Bryant family gave me a peek into another way of living

Living in Brooklyn with my mother and two younger brothers.

Nevertheless, on one occasion we did have a party. One of the guests, a boyfriend of Aunt Rose, my father's younger sister, played ragtime on our piano. I was thrilled, thrilled. My older cousin, Irving Herman, was there too. I must have been three or four because I ran over to Irving expecting him to pick me up. Instead he gave me the knee, my first sampling of rejection. It wasn't pleasant, but it was a learning experience.

On another occasion, Mrs. Reitman, a close friend of my mother's, dropped in with another lady one afternoon. I was home alone but suggested that they come in, as my mother would surely be back soon. I served them tea. I can only write that this literally happened. I must have been ten or eleven. As I look back, it now seems to have been such an extraordinary thing to do. Obviously, I was compensating; we did not entertain. I did have one birthday party when I was six. I remember, as you probably also do, playing "Musical Chairs," "Pin the Tail on the Donkey," and "Spin the Bottle." If the bottle pointed to me, I could select a girl to kiss. Ruth Bornman was my choice and, in retrospect, I suppose she was my first crush.

436 Franklin Avenue: The Beginning

Ruth Bornman invited me to her sixth birthday party. She also lived on Quincy Street in an elegant townhouse that provided me with my second entrance to an upscale home. The high point of the party was squeezing Ruth into a small space between the upright piano and the corner and kissing her on the cheek.

In 1916 anti-Semitism was part of growing up in Brooklyn; mindless for the most part, based on a given that the Jews were "Christ killers." Eleven-year-old McHenry, Mac for short, went to the Catholic school on Madison Street, just around the corner. Mac was the block's bully, and Morty was a Jew, as well as being an especially soft touch. I don't understand bullies. Inflicting pain should be repellent because no one likes to suffer. Yet, bullies are worldwide, and Mac rated four stars. He was very strong, could chin the bar thirty times; I could chin the bar only three times. Some of us used the YMCA gym. One afternoon as we left the Y, Mac cornered me and challenged me to a fight. There was no way out. I said, "I'll fight you tomorrow after school at 3:30."

The next day, like a lamb led to slaughter, I went to face my doom. I had one unexpected bit of help from Wally Reid, who also lived on Madison Street. Wally was a WASP but, for whatever reason, (fair play?) volunteered to be my second. Otherwise I was alone, facing a ring of some forty Catholic kids gathered in a circle to watch the slaughter. We were using fists and squared off. Mac immediately charged me like the bull he was. Both of his arms revolving in "vertical circles" like two propellers turned sideways, all I had to do was put out my fist and let him run into it. After that first hit, I realized Mac's face was totally unprotected, so I started punching. This was such an astonishing surprise: Mac knew nothing about boxing. I knew nothing either, but obviously more than he. I used two fists, knocked out two of his front teeth and blackened both eyes. The bully was craven – he surrendered. Mac stayed home for two days, ashamed to come out, disfigured as he was.

Those nasty kids, those bad sports, then asked me to fight Tom Allen, the middle one of the three Allen brothers. My friend Wally said I was obligated to fight only Mac; we had won the fight fairly, and I walked away with my head up. Now here's the funny part. Even though I had beaten Mac so badly, I was still afraid; but the bullying was over, he too was afraid.

I was, of course, pleased with myself, actually quite proud. Several days later, two boys from Putnam Avenue, around the other corner, came by to see the Jewish fighter. One kid said, "So you're the guy who beat McHenry." I said, "Yes," and he dealt me a blow to the belly and walked away leaving me gasping.

My parents, for a short time employed three or four girls to do things with red feathers. As I think about it now, it is quite possible that they used those red feathers to make flowers or fans. The fact is, I just don't know. I don't know what they made and I don't know to whom the feathers were sold. In 1918, our large kitchen had been converted into a small craft workshop. It was the one time we had money, some money, enough to hire Eva Braverman as an all-around housemaid. Actually, she was probably given to us by her family who couldn't afford to keep her. I believe Eva came to us for little more than room and board.

So Eva Braverman was next, and that was almost the real thing. I slept in a double bed with my brother. A double bed in the adjoining room was shared by my mother and father. That was the parlor floor (the second floor), and a cot was set up for Eva in the parlor. Eva must have been thirteen or fourteen because she was just beginning to have pubic hair. On two occasions when my mother and father were out, Eva and I engaged in sexual intercourse to the extent that was possible with an eleven-year-old; which, for me, was not possible. Mother must have discovered what had been going on, because Eva was terminated. This time, too, I received no punishment.

I was almost twelve when the red feather business, whatever it was, evidently laid an egg, because we had to move. I left behind an assortment of experiences: playing host for Mrs. Reitman, being introduced to the pains of anti-Semitism, my incredible victory in a fist fight, and pre-adolescent sex with Eva Braverman.

2

Adolescence: I Become a Circus Bareback Rider

In 1919, we moved to a rental apartment at 308 Lincoln Road with three bedrooms, a dining room, a parlor, a kitchen, and a bath for $50 a month. It was a genteel Protestant neighborhood. My father began what I believe was a new venture. Unfortunately, I do not know and never knew how he came to it. In fact, there were two new ventures in our family. And that, temporarily at least, was how we could pay the rent – both ventures were located in Luna Park.

Luna Park was Coney Island's bid for the elite; it was Coney Island's bright spot and it was world famous. If there ever was a fairyland, it might have looked like Luna Park. There was an admission charge and a charge for each individual ride. People paid the price because Luna Park was so, so beautiful. The park was built around a small pond and Luna Park's white tower. The tower had only one function: to dazzle people. It was snow white from bottom to top and decorated with a series of twenty-four-inch circles, each containing colored bulbs, a lighting display that was Luna's equivalent of Times Square, but aesthetically, even more satisfying –no commercials. I loved it with all my heart and I can see it in my mind's eye now. On the last night of each season, the park's personnel gathered around the tower while the band played "Auld Lang Syne." The tower's medallions were turned off two or three at a time and at the final note of the song, the tower was dark. It always brought tears to my eyes.

The park had the usual attractions: Dragon's Gorge, the scenic railway, a roller coaster, the crazy house, the tunnel of love, the water mill ride, the whip, the tumbler, and its most famous attraction, "Shoot the Chutes." The "Chutes" was a Luna Park exclusive. "Shoot the Chutes" was a wonder to watch and it was fascinating, vibrating with life. Picture a ski jump, double the length, and quadruple the width; wide enough to hold two oversized rowboats side by side with some space in between. The entire chute was covered with running water, interrupted intermittently by metal pieces twelve inches wide and one inch high. The metal pieces were placed crosswise, which created a series of tiny waterfalls.

The entrance to the ride was at the pond where six people stepped into a good-sized rowboat. The boat was moved onto a constantly revolving cable, a chain that made a lovely noise as it pulled the rowboat to the top of the chute. The chain was stopped, the rowboat turned and moved onto a track. The guide released the boat, which then zoomed down the waterfalls at full speed, ending in a big splash at the pond. A man then hooked the boat. I loved the noise of the cables, the water, and the spectator fun of standing on the bridge and watching the second rowboat, with its six screaming occupants, roaring down the chute. The water-covered slope was beautiful and vibrant. The boat wound up with an enormous splash as it hit the pond. I was twelve years old.

The usual fairground games were also part of Luna Park's allure. Knock down three bottles with a baseball, and win a baby doll. Better yet, "drop the man in the water" by hitting him in the head. To stay dry, and/or to avoid injury, the man had to duck the ball by moving his head. Then, of course, there was the shooting gallery, and next to that was my father's stand, featuring two minuscule bowling alleys. The alleys were two and a half feet wide, six feet long, and came up to my waist. Three small pins were held upright by strings going through a hole underneath each pin. After they were knocked down, my father pulled a lever to stand them back up. The ball fell into a sack at the end of the alley to avoid rebounding. My father demonstrated how easy it was to knock down the three pins with the ball. Ah, but there were two balls in the sack. My father took the bigger one for demonstrations then gave the smaller one to customers.

After the customer lost enough money, my father handed him a compensation prize so he could walk away with something, still wondering why he couldn't knock down the pins. Father's deception made me very uncomfortable but I never made it an issue.

Adolescence: I Become a Circus Bareback Rider

Luna Park also had a one-ring circus that was free, covered by the admission charge out front. The circus was located at the far end of the park, encouraging people to pass all the attractions, including my father's stand.

My parents had another business, if you could call it that. My mother would sit at a small, round table, alone in Luna Park, making imitation jewelry, and Aunt Anna, my mother's younger sister, would do the same thing. Aunt Anna had her stand in Feltman's Beer Garden, directly opposite Luna Park, between the boardwalk and Surf Avenue, Coney Island's Broadway.

Men and women would walk by, stop, look, and from time to time, buy the ladies' brooches, bow knots, forget-me-nots, rosettes, and tiaras, all made by hand. The work was called filigree. They used two kinds of fine colored wire for the brooches and all work was crafted while the customer was watching – that was the gimmick. The tiaras were made of a different kind of wire, sparkling like diamonds, until they tarnished.

One afternoon, the bareback rider in the Luna Park circus (also the owner) offered me a job – $3 a show, learning how to become a bareback rider. I said, "Yes." Gee, mom I'm an actor. He strapped me into a leather harness attached to a thin wire cable hoisting me onto the back of a horse. The cable followed the horse around the ring. He instructed us (there were two of us, one for the day show and the other for the night show) about how to stay on. If we fell off, the harness prevented us from getting hurt. To make the act funny, he would make it impossible for us to stay on in different ways. I enjoyed my work as a performer but it was cut short by the law. One night after the show, I was arrested, taken to a prison for children, and held as a material witness against my boss, who was charged with employing a minor. At thirteen, I could not get working papers; one had to be fourteen. A burly matron ordered me into a bathtub with instructions to wash myself thoroughly, including my hair. It was now 2:00 in the morning and she was not in a good mood. She came into the bathroom just as I stood up to grab for the towel. I was deeply embarrassed and plopped down into the tub, taking the towel with me. She gave me a whack on the head and said, "This is no playground; we cannot afford to waste towels." I was taken to a dormitory with about thirty beds.

It was the middle of the night and the dormitory was dark except for one low, shaded red bulb. For me, it was quite frightening. There was no empty bed so I had to share a cot with a boy whose head was covered with a white skullcap – lice. Needless to say, I couldn't sleep. Fortunately, a friend of the family had me released on bail the next afternoon. I do not think of this as a live-and-learn experience, rather as a look into life's sleazier side.

My mother insisted that I go to Boy's High School, a thirty-five-minute ride on my bike. Erasmus Hall was Brooklyn's Ivy League High School (almost). It was co-ed and only a few blocks from our home but Boy's High had a high scholastic standing (it was for nerds), and mother thought I was a student. Mother was wrong; I was no student.

Boy's High obviously had no girls, and I was not happy in that environment. If I had gone to Erasmus Hall, I might possibly have achieved a diploma. Although I seldom did homework in elementary school, I had no problem getting passing grades. But I found high school frightening. We were obliged to choose elective courses. And, as I really was not a student, I had no idea what courses to select. At elementary school, we stayed in one classroom but in high school each subject was in a different room. That, too, put me off balance.

Right off, I was forced to study Latin and expected to conjugate Latin verbs. I knew no one who spoke Latin, so why should I learn to speak it? I flunked first-term Latin twice and had to drop it. A foreign language was mandatory, so I switched to French. I knew no one who spoke French either, and thought it to be a stupid language. You couldn't say seventy-nine; you had to say sixty plus ten plus nine (soixante dix-neuf). And that's not all. Inanimate objects are arbitrarily given a gender; a table was a she, a chair was a he. For all I know, either one might both be "he" or "she." It was just too silly and, to make it worse, the adjectives had to match the gender. So I flunked first-term French twice. Then I flunked first-term Spanish. I was friendless; no baseball, no football, no basketball, no hockey, and there were those miserable grades. Yet, I did have one minute of glory.

I played second violin in the school orchestra, confident that the other violins smothered my incorrect notes. Nevertheless, I was privileged to play a solo for the assembly. The orchestra's conductor accompanied me on the piano. When I finished playing my piece, "Traumerei," he whispered, "I've never heard a bluff like you." He was saying, in effect, that my technique was not up to the feeling I had for the music – not that he thought of it in those terms.

I was sixteen and dropped out. Mother needed the money because my father's income was sporadic, if it came at all. Flunking out of high school created one serious problem. I had concluded, based on the evidence of my impossible grades, that I was stupid.

Aunt Anna was a bright spot. She loved me and was endlessly generous with her affection. She never married and I never knew her to have a boyfriend. Aunt Anna gave me my first dancing lesson. It must have taken place at Grandma's (maternal), because Grandma had a Victrola. Aunt Anna was no dancer but she showed me the fundamentals of the box step. It was some five years later that my kid brother Ray showed me the fundamentals of the Lindy Hop and I danced for the very first time with a Girl Scout at a block party. Years later, when I made my first visit to the Roseland Ballroom, I discovered that I was a "dancer" with a high-level aptitude that I had not been aware of. I had rhythm, I still have rhythm, and I still love to dance.

Beatrice, a second cousin, lived on Eastern Parkway, one of Brooklyn's better sections. Beatrice invited me to her sweet sixteen birthday party and introduced me to her group of friends. As I had no such group, I became a marginal member of hers. The leader was a boy who actually had a poor complexion. I was so out of it that I thought maybe I too should become "pimply." How could I have been so stupid, so desperate, to even think it? But I did.

I am relating this seemingly pointless episode to remind myself of the starting point. How far can one's self-confidence drop?

"Skookie" Schoonmaker, a boy I knew in the neighborhood, invited me to go along to his high school prom. It was there that I fell deeply in love. Perhaps I should amend that. I had an immediate, crashing crush on Julia Kelller. Julia had laughing eyes; they closed up when she laughed. She wore a stunning black and white plaid taffeta dress that was utterly becoming. A small group of us went to a

Chinese restaurant after the music stopped. My crush had to be put on hold because, as it turned out, Julia looked right through me. There was no room for me in her life.

When I was twenty I ran into her again. By then I had my fancy little aluminum two-seater Essex and a lot more confidence. Julia was friendlier.

3

In 1923, I Begin a "Non-Career"

When I was fourteen, I received papers that legally permitted me to work. I found my first summer job in the Woolworth building by going to the top floor, the fifty-fourth, and walking my way down from floor to floor. Obviously, I was a boy destined for high places. In 1921, the Woolworth building was the world's tallest. On the forty-ninth floor, the Wah Chang Trading Corporation hired me as an office boy. They paid me eight dollars a week, with no tax deductions. I gave the entire salary to my mother, who gave me fifty cents a day. The subway to New York was five cents each way, leaving me forty cents to spend, two cents of which were used to buy the Daily News. I was a brown bagger; I always brought lunch to the office.

In July 1923, I found my first full-time job at J. W. Davis & Company Stockbrokers at 115 Broadway. Mr. Saunders took me on as an office boy. Right after Christmas, I asked to see him. "Mr. Saunders," I said, "I really don't understand your business." Coming from out of nowhere, I continued, "I need to be in a business where I have something in my hand and I sell it to someone for a profit." I did not tell Mr. Saunders that my other reason for leaving was the mindless anti-Semitism that prevailed in the back office bookkeeping cage.

The anti-Semitism was not the equivalent of Hitler's war on the Jews or of the Southerners active abuse of the Blacks. Anti-Semitism made itself evident with "Rabbi" jokes, which made the rounds of the office staff.

Mother's friend, Mrs. Reitman, suggested that I try the textile firms located in the Fourth Avenue area, now known as Park Avenue South. Once again I started at the top floor of a building, this time on the corner of Twenty-sixth Street. At the eighth floor I became discouraged and decided to try another building, but the elevator door opened on the seventh floor and I caught a glimpse of a fabric display. I stayed on the elevator and went back up to the seventh floor. Manny Harris hired me to work in the showroom. The name of the firm was Erlanger-Blumgart. It was January of 1924 and my salary was $14 a week.

Cyrus Sulzberger was chairman of the board and there were three other senior executives. It was, in one sense, a house divided. Louis Portong was vice president in charge of the Everfast Wash Fabrics division, introducing cottons that were colorfast. The firm also had velvets, velveteens, and "Earlglow Linings" (rayon, the first synthetic) used to line women's coats and men's jackets (President Seiferheld's division).

My job was to help salesmen take care of customers in the showroom. The line was varied and cumbersome and, from time to time, I had to bring out actual pieces from the piece goods department so that customers could more accurately gauge the quality. Customers usually ordered sample cuts - three to six yards of a solid color fabric and/or several printed fabrics of various patterns - and the company then made samples. If the samples looked promising the customers placed their orders. Incidentally, I also made all of those sample cuts.

I must have been something of a clown because I was reprimanded many times by Harry Harris, the office manager. The head of the department, however, took it out on Harry. He was relentless and in my naïve mind, he represented the "boss," the businessman. Years later, when I hired my first employee, I told him I didn't want to be a businessman, a "boss", and would retire in five years. But my early towel fights in the men's room and similar immature activities resulted in many warnings to me, about eleven in all. On this particular day I knew the warnings were over because I was now called into the office of the chairman, Cyrus Sulzberger. He said, "Mortie, we can no longer keep you on as you are demoralizing the entire seventh floor. (The sixth floor was for stock and shipping). Evidently, you don't take our business seriously."

I said, "Mr. Sulzberger, how can you say that I don't take Everfast seriously when Everfast is to cotton fabrics what Wrigley is to chewing gum?" That unexpected extemporaneous remark caused Mr. Sulzberger to reconsider. He said, "Well, we cannot have you working in-house but maybe we can make an experiment, try you out as a salesman." I knew what that was like because I had carried Tom Platt's bags when he went calling on customers in the city.

New York City was free territory except for those accounts already listed by the two senior salesmen in the city, Victor Loeb and Sam Wolf. I followed my usual procedure by going to the top of the building that listed manufacturers and then walking down floor by floor. That's how I found my first big account. Seaver Brothers was not on anyone's list. Velveteen was new and just becoming fashionable. They bought small yardage to make sample dresses. When I returned to the office that afternoon, Belle Murray, the telephone operator, said, "Mortie, everybody's talking about you." It never occurred to me to ask why or what were they saying. The thought that anyone could be talking about me, a nobody, was overwhelming. Me? They were talking about me?

David Sulzberger, Cyrus's son, was the new sales manager. He was a most attractive man whom I very much admired. Victor Loeb said, "David, Jeff Seaver is a member of my golf club. That kid can't handle an account of that size." David called me in and explained that even though Seaver Brothers was not on Victor Loeb's list, he had to take the account away from me because Mr. Seaver was a member of Mr. Loeb's golf club. I didn't think that was exactly right but I did not put up a fuss. Subsequently, a second account was taken away. Fortunately, I still retained the three other large accounts I had uncovered. Although I was able to live very comfortably on those three accounts, I had been totally demoralized. All motivation was gone.

Lee Cohen was a new friend. I was eighteen and Lee was all of twenty-two, handsome and a womanizer with nothing else on his mind. His father owned a Lincoln sedan and, if the family was not using it, Lee was permitted to borrow the car on a Friday or Saturday. Not having any dates, we'd go "cruisin' for cooze." Eastern Parkway was Brooklyn's premier boulevard, starting at the Grand Army Plaza and going past the Brooklyn Botanical Garden and the Brooklyn Museum of Art, a tree-lined boulevard, an elegant place for promenading. We went out, like fishermen, trying to pick up girls our age who were dateless and promenading. Although I participated, it was most demeaning. I have nothing good to say for it except possibly that it gave me the synthetic thrill that hunters and fishermen share.

Lee and I became partners in a sailing canoe that we kept at the Mic Mac Canoe Club in Sheepshead Bay. Sailing for me was a new and most gratifying experience. It was nature at its best. Looking back, it was akin to skiing; gravity created movement on skis, wind created movement in a sailboat. The wonder of it was that even if the wind blew in only one direction, we could sail our boat in all four directions. I really loved sailing. The experience of being moved without a motor, of harnessing the wind was wonderful. It was the aesthetics of nature that moved me.

We entered a race starting in Staten Island and ending in Sheepshead Bay. All of us were towed to Staten Island, where the race would start. It was beautiful to see all the canoes beached one alongside the other with sails flapping. There were about thirty entries. We were all lined up, the starting gun was fired, and we were off. Halfway home we were hit by a fierce squall and more than half the boats capsized, but we held one of the few that remained upright. The storm was followed by a calm, and a good half hour was spent listlessly waiting. Then, as might be expected, we caught a breeze and sailed triumphantly into our marina. I received a copper Survivor's Medal. To me it looked like gold. It's been in my handkerchief drawer for some seventy-three years.

Lee Cohen, my sailing partner
introduced me to Victor Thall III
(The III was phony).

Victor Thall III and Mona, his wife
on the Coney Island boardwalk.

Late one afternoon, after we put our boat away, we were talking on the dock - Lee and I and his friend, Victor Thal III (the III was phony, Victor wasn't even a Junior). He was painter, an artist who had recently come back from two years in Paris. While we were talking, a thunderstorm pelted us. Lee said, "God is acting up again," and I said, "I don't believe there is a God." Victor was more sophisticated and said, "Mortie, if you think there is no God, then just say that to God and then dive in the water in the middle of this lighting. I dare you." I was trembling when I looked to the sky and said, "If there is a God up there, strike me dead when I hit the water," and dove in. A profound experience it was not, but on that day, I became a certified atheist.

We named our canoe "Maxine" for Lee's girlfriend, Maxine Masters. Maxine had a friend named Carol Shlumbeger. We had a date to take the girls sailing. We beached our canoe at Orient Point, spread out our blanket, and after the sun went down, at the age of eighteen, I experienced for the first time the sensation of sexual intercourse. It was aesthetically sublime, heaven realized. It is beyond my ability to describe it, but if you're over fifteen, you probably have already experienced it. You don't need my description, other than it being a moment I remember to this day.

Perhaps I should include the low point. My mother and father were out of town at the Port Jefferson Fair and my two younger brothers were with Grandma. So at Lee's suggestion the four of us - Lee and Maxine, Carol and I - had sex together in our double bed. Too much of a good thing put an end to paradise. Thinking back on it produces a "yecch." Live and learn. This is not the whole story of my sex life, but for the purposes of this memoir, it's about all you're going to get.

I was earning the equivalent of forty-five thousand in today's dollars. I was almost nineteen, single, and able to buy my first secondhand car, a two-seater Essex roadster built to look like a racing car. It was a flashy piece of junk that I bought from a mechanic for $125, but it did run, and it brought me the company of Sally Anson. She was eighteen when she gave me permission to take her virginity. She had what, I presume, would be considered a perfect female body but I was appalled to discover there was no sex appeal. I could look at her in all her beautiful nakedness, only to find my usual passionate response lacking. That may be a slight exaggeration, because she did become pregnant. She knew someone who had a friend who would do an illegal abortion for $400 in cash. I gave Sally the money and the problem was uncomfortably resolved. Oh, how many things I didn't know. Among which, and most importantly, was learning the importance of chemistry, that invisible sexual attraction.

Some years later, I was twenty-three when I met Alice Moritz. Alice was a saleswoman/model in a relatively small firm that manufactured expensive ladies' coats. Alice was, in my eyes, breathtakingly beautiful, with laughing eyes and an enchanting presence. She was not a baby doll; she was, shall I say, "for real." I lived in Brooklyn and Alice lived in the Bronx. Her parents were Swiss, her father, a piano tuner for Steinway. Fortunately, my Aunt Pauline, my mother's youngest sister, lived in the Bronx not too far from Alice. She was not averse to setting up a cot when I elected to bypass the long drive back to Brooklyn.

Alice and I were made for each other – there were no low points, no arguments, and no political differences. I was deeply infatuated, although I never said I loved her. On one occasion, one of many, we went to the Paramount Theater. This was well before the days that Frank Sinatra, Jerry Lewis, and Dean Martin headed up the Paramount stage shows that always preceded a feature film. In 1930, the stage shows consisted of jugglers, acrobats, exotic dancers, and chorus girl routines. The Paramount was a most elaborate theater, inspired somewhat by Saint Peter's Cathedral in Rome. It was a half an hour before the show broke, so we went downstairs to their luxurious lounge to pass the time. A small booth had been installed where, for one dollar, one could make a recording. Alice said, "Mortie, let's make a record." (I was "Mortie" until 1943. When I opened the Mortimer Levitt Gallery I became Mortimer.) I said, "Fine, but what can we do? We can't sing, and we must do something."

Alice said, "Recite a poem." I said, "I don't know a poem." She said, "Write one." I said, "I can't write a poem." She said, "Of course you can. Do it." And so I did:

For Alice:

> *To attempt*
>
> *To show a bent,*
>
> *For a talent*
>
> *Which I haven't,*
>
> *Seems to imply*
>
> *That even I've,*
>
> *become a fool*
>
>
> *But after all*
>
> *I'm only human,*
>
> *And being human*
>
> *I'm being sane,*

When cause of you, dear

I wax inane.

Perhaps I could be a model?

I had a mad crush on Alice, yet could
not consider marriage.

It's silly, I know, but I was so proud of my poem that from time to time I actually recite it, mainly to myself. In the same way, I also recite, "In the middle of the night, Miss Clavell turned on the light, and said, 'Something is not right,'" from *Madeline*, Bemelman's charming book for children.

Alice and I enjoyed an easygoing relationship, although we never slept together (this was 1930). We had been seeing each other for some eight months. I had never been inside her family's apartment and she had never been in my home in Brooklyn or my aunt's apartment in the Bronx. On this particular evening we were saying goodnight at her door. Alice said, "Mortie don't you think it is time for us to talk about marriage?" I was taken aback because there had been no prelude, it just came out of the blue.

I said, "Frankly Alice, I've never thought about marriage because I am a nothing. I'm absolutely nothing. Yet I know, I just know that one day, my big chance will come. When that happens, I cannot be held back by a wife." Alice said, "Mortie, I understand. Get yourself another date for New Year's Eve." In that instant the floor gave away and I fell through the hole, or at least that's what it felt like. I had no defense, because I knew she was right (if you're going to jump, jump). I carried the torch for a whole year except for fifteen time-stopping minutes on Christmas Eve.

Kane-Weill, one of my three big accounts, invited me to their annual Christmas party. They manufactured expensive ladies sportswear. After the party, the sales manager, Tom Bronson, invited me and two of their models, to his apartment for a nightcap. I was almost twenty-four but had never been inside anyone's home in Manhattan. Tom lived on Central Park West and through a window I could see an electric sign displaying the time and weather. We all had a drink together before he turned off the lights. I don't remember Tom's girl, but mine was Mary Carter. We knew each other because I had been in their showroom so many times, though we had never dated.

In that lovely, never-to-be-forgotten apartment on Christmas Eve, Mary permitted me to forget Alice. It is easy to recall because in the middle of making love I could see that electric weather sign changing, and I kept thinking to myself, "At last I'm free of Alice." I was mistaken, grossly mistaken. The next day found me still missing Alice as though Mary had never happened. Mary was lovely, nice to be with, but she wasn't Alice. I vowed, then and there, that I would never again permit myself to become *so* vulnerable.

I seldom went to the office in the morning, claiming to be out visiting customers. I would get to New York usually in time for lunch "with the boys," Nat Levi and the Pretzfeld twins, Jim and Dick. Wednesday afternoon there was matinee dancing at Roseland and I would take the afternoon off. Sometimes I would go to an afternoon show at the Paramount or at Radio City Music Hall. I must have had a pleasing personality because the few accounts I had always gave me a warm welcome.

Friendships with men were few and far between, especially in my "growing up days." George Howard was a man who, at the time, had engendered some level of respect. He was pleasant looking, understated, laid back, and interesting in a quiet way; a stockbroker-to-be. I met him through his sister. On several occasions, George and I double dated. In 1931, I read an article in Time Magazine about nudist camps and suggested to George that it might be fun to go. The camp was located in New Jersey, fifty miles due west of the Lincoln Tunnel, as it turned out, just four miles away from the New Jersey factory I built years later in 1951. Mr. Soshinisky, a Russian and a health nut, was the proprietor.

The rates were reasonable for bed and board, three meals a day, swimming, volleyball, and conversation. All activities centered on a small, very clean pond, the water being constantly fed by a small stream. So, what's it like to take your clothes off in public? Not at all what one might expect. And erections, if any, were never visible. Actually, there was a good reason for that. Nudity gives one an incredible sense of freedom, overwhelming and totally unexpected. To experience it is the only way to understand it.

Soshinisky's camp was in large measure for families; perhaps that's an exaggeration, since there were only four couples with children. Newcomers are interesting until they take their clothes off. When the clothes are off, we are all one, nudists. I recall only two women, and only one who really had style. She walked around naked wearing a stylish black hat, makeup, a black patent leather belt, an over-the-shoulder black pouch bag, and black pubic hair. She was smashing and she was fun to talk with. She was there with her husband. I have no recollection of the husband. The other girl was fifteen or sixteen. She had come with her mother and father, who dutifully took off their clothes, but the daughter was not to be persuaded. Overnight she evidently had a change of heart and the next morning came to the pond unclothed. Volleyball was the one sport in which most of the members participated. After watching them play, one had to conclude that breasts and penises look better trussed when engaging in physical sports.

Having stayed at Soshinisky's camp twice, we decided to go to a neighboring camp that was mainly for singles. Camp Sunshine had none of Soshinisky's integrity. It did not espouse any fabled improvement in health. It was just a nudist camp with the pond and the usual volleyball court. The campers were, socially, a small step down from Soshinsky's. On my first afternoon I remember a short conversation with Iris, not very interesting, but a conversation nevertheless. An Irish girl, she had a pale freckled-face, was several years older than I, and two-inches taller.

Curiously, I had a room to myself. That night when I was undressing (we wore clothes at night), the door was open and Iris walked in. She sat down and we talked for a while as I finished undressing and got into bed. The room was lit with an overhead bulb and I asked Iris to throw the wall switch off on the way out. I was fast asleep, awakened by Iris, who had slipped into my bed, under my sheets, and nestled we were like two soup spoons. Something like that could happen only in a dream, but this was no dream. Was it exciting? Oh, my God, yes! But let's get back to my non-career.

"Everfast Ed" (Edgar Rosenberg) should have been my role model. He might have been if David Sulzberger had not taken away my motivation. Edgar's territory was New England. However, on two occasions, Everfast Ed called on New York City accounts and I carried his bags. He wanted our entire line and he showed his customer everything. In contrast, I carried only one tenth of the line. Edgar was relentless, charming, well groomed, and he seldom took "no" for an answer. He handled all our samples with grace –as a jeweler might when showing a diamond ring. His nails were manicured. He was immaculate and all business. Edgar showed me what it was like to be a salesman, a real salesman. I never became that kind of a salesman and it was only a matter of time before my immature behavior caught up with me. After twelve years I was terminated. It was January of 1936.

I had a stable income but was doing nothing to recruit new business. David Sulzberger believed, and rightly so, that a salesman should be exploiting the whole market with no excuse for coasting. Ameritex, our major competitor, took me on immediately. Lucky me!

4

My First Wife: The Glamorous Anna Fleisher Friede

I was twenty-nine when Nat Levi, bless him, introduced me to Annie. Nat also introduced me to skiing and to his boss, Jerry Rossman, the president of Ameritex, Everfast's number one competitor. Nat (*The telephone just rang – Nat is dead*) invited Annie to join our all-male luncheon table. Her left arm was in a sling, due to a broken collarbone. She had been horseback riding when her horse shied, and off she went.

Annie and I hit it off immediately. She was a handsome girl with a strong face, good cheekbones, brown eyes, and a strong nose. She spoke with an attractive Bennington College accent. Annie was temporarily living at the Chelsea Hotel, a hotel patronized by authors, agents, and publishers. Shortly after our meeting, Annie moved into her own apartment at 91 Charles Street in Greenwich Village; an enormous corner room with five floor-to-ceiling windows, a kitchenette, and a bath. At the time, I was still an unheralded salesman.

This was 1936, and Communism was just becoming fashionable. Annie was a liberal and an activist. Her father, Walter "Wally" Fleisher, was an engineer and an inventor specializing in humidifiers, a Philadelphia mainliner, as mainline as possible for a Jew. The machine he had invented did double duty, taking moisture out of the air and cooling it at the same time without refrigeration.

Annie's parents were divorced. Her mother, Aline, a talented textile designer and a "grand dame" in every respect, had married Arthur Garfield Hayes, an internationally respected lawyer with a bank balance to match. Hayes was co-counsel with Clarence Darrow at the Scope's Trial (The Monkey Trial) and later represented the United States at the Reichstag Trials.

Annie had recently been divorced from Donald Friede. His firm, Covicci-Friede, was John Steinbeck's publisher. Friede, a sophisticated bon vivant who had inherited his wealth, loved good wine, gourmet food, good clothes, and women. I never asked Annie why they divorced.

I couldn't understand how a woman as sophisticated as Annie, well born and well bred, could be interested in someone like me. I still lived with my mother and two younger brothers in Brooklyn and no longer had any interest in my career. In the 1930's, it was not customary for children to break away on their own, even in their twenties. Well, it turned out that Annie was totally won over by my unexpected candor. But that was only for starters – there was also the chemistry, another one of life's small mysteries. Annie said, "Mortie, you are the sweetest smelling man I have ever known." We became a couple almost immediately.

Annie brought me into a world of awe, a world of authors, journalists, and publishers, a world I had subconsciously yearned for, despite the fact that I flunked out of high school. However, its sophistication could be quite confusing as in an incident that took place before we were married: One night I was in the bathtub at Annie's Charles Street apartment. There was a loud banging on the door and I heard Annie yell, "Max, go away. I have company." But Max refused to go away and continued pounding on the door with all his strength. Annie called out, "Mortie, what shall I do?" I said, "Let him in. I'll put on a robe."

It was Max Lerner, a well-known political columnist for the *New York Post*. This was at a time when the *Post* was in its prime. Max was not a handsome man, but undoubtedly attractive - short and dynamic, with an enormous ego. As a former lover, he seemed to feel he had marital rights. We spent a pleasant half an hour together while he slowly realized that he had been replaced.

To my astonishment, as time moved on, it became apparent that Annie was actually thinking about marriage. Although I was delighted to have Annie as a girlfriend, I did not have the mad crush I had had on Alice. I didn't profess to love Annie; I didn't even think of that word "love." It is a word that I cannot use casually, and I never even used it with Alice. Yet Annie seemed to be everything I could ever want in a woman. She was born into another world and married into yet another world, a world of the intelligentsia. Annie was indeed a woman of substance. I thought to myself that if I didn't marry Annie, there must be something <u>wrong</u> with me, meaning, that I would never get married. That was frightening though it was a small example of looking directly to the bottom line.

The thought that there might be something wrong with me was scary. Actually, I undervalued the main point, namely, that my feeling for Annie fell short of what could be called love. It in no way equaled the feeling I later had for Mimi, my second wife, to whom, for the first time, I felt free to say, "I love you." There was another thing about Annie; she was an activist, a militant activist, and very knowledgeable about Communism. She inducted me into the world of government and to top it off, the byways of psychoanalysis, a word which until then had not even been in my vocabulary.

I look motivated but motivation is gone.

Looking back, I see that I lived through some historical moments. In 1929, I was one of a hoard of wise guy investors, putting money into the stock market, buying stocks based on the advice of my broker (big laugh), going on hot tips, always buying stocks that were heavily margined. In 1929, I was cleaned out in that monstrous stock market crash. In 1932, having not benefited from my earlier experience, I was cleaned out again, and shamefully but typically, I was cleaned out yet again in 1937. After that third sock in the eye, I, a militant atheist, turned my eyes to the heavens and said out loud, "Dear God, I'll never again put a cent into the stock market. Never again!"

I also lived through the Depression without realizing its historical significance. It is probable that I was still reading the *Daily News*. I read those headlines about the big hitters who committed suicide by jumping out of windows but I didn't need those headlines to see what was happening. I could see my peers selling apples on street corners. Fortunately, I survived the Depression without scars.

For that matter, I had also lived through the First World War, again without scars, although I do remember the victory parade. Mother took me to New York so we could both witness it. Back home in Brooklyn I started a poem:

The War is over at last and

our boys are coming home

The ships are sailing fast

to their goal of home sweet home ...

That's as far as I got with my poem, so it was quickly evident that I had no aptitude as a poet. Incidentally, I realize that I also lived through the Flapper Age, Clara Bow (the "it" girl) and F. Scott Fitzgerald's *The Great Gatsby*. For me, it was never "The Roaring Twenties" or "The Jazz Age." I was never a history major.

After some eight months of dating, Annie and I decided to get married at City Hall. One Saturday morning, the day we had decided upon for the marriage ceremony, Annie said, "Before I make breakfast, I want you to go out and buy me a gardenia corsage." Annie, like Mimi, had style, the kind of style I lacked and still lack (although there may have been some modest improvements).

We had already gone to City Hall and filled out our application. That morning there was one couple before us. When it came our turn, the secretary, who also acted as witness, brought us to an inner office, stood us before a makeshift bower, and introduced us to the "marrier." This was a time when Tammany Hall, a corrupt branch of the Democratic Party, ruled New York City politics. *The Journal*, a Hearst newspaper more notable for scandal than news, frequently had a cartoon featuring a typical Tammany Hall politico, overweight and with white hair, a bulbous nose from too much alcohol, and a heavy gold chain stretched across the vest holding a gold watch in his vest-pocket. And it was this character, this caricature, this symbol of corruption, who was to perform this serious, sacred, and for me, very frightening ceremony.

It was frightening because I took marriage seriously – it was a gargantuan step. So, when this Tammany politico told us to hold hands and began the ceremony in his most unctuous tones, it struck me as sacrilegious, ludicrous, and ironic; it was more than I could handle. I broke into a burst of wildly hysterical, uncontrollable laughter. The "marrier" said, "It's people like you, coming here drunk, that gives City Hall marriages a bad name," and turning to his secretary said, "Give Mr. Levitt his $2." I said, "Excuse me, sir, but I'm not drunk. Smell." I blew directly into his face. "As a matter of fact, I am a teetotaler. I don't drink at all, but I am nervous and I am very serious, and we do want very much to be married. Please, please don't send us away." He agreed to perform the ceremony and started all over again by saying, "Please join hands." It was very, very hard for me to prevent another outburst.

I did it by keeping my eye on the main point:: simply, that we were there to get married. We left his unromantic offices and went to two phone booths. I phoned my mother to let her know, and Annie phoned her mother who invited us to come over directly for lunch. The cook made us an elegant lunch and the maid wore white gloves when she served. That afternoon I took Annie to the Roseland Ballroom – from the sublime to the ridiculous.

I don't know why I took my new wife there but I just hadn't planned ahead (no style?). I should be ashamed and I am squirming as I write this. Good God, I was indeed nothing, impossibly unsophisticated. Annie had never been to Roseland, so for her, it was something of a novelty, a look into another world. Freddie, a bellhop, and one of Roseland's champion ballroom dancers, toasted us with a beer at the bar. The next day we had a champagne lunch at the elegant home of Annie's aunt, her father's sister, in North Salem, New York's Westchester County. Thus began our marriage.

Annie's world was far from the one I had known; serious people, intellectuals, who also lived "high on the hog." Wally Fleisher, Annie's father and his second wife, an editor, lived in New City, Rockland County. Rockland County was the scene of Edmund Wilson's novel, *Hecate County*. There was an interesting enclave of people in the arts, in theater, in music, in writing, in painting, and, not to be overlooked, in advertising. Edmund Wilson, Burgess Meredith, John Houseman, Helen Hayes, and her husband, Ben Hecht, were neighbors and friends of Wally's. Wally had a charming house built alongside their lovely pond, clean, and deep enough to place a diving board at one end.

Arthur Garfield Hayes, who had married Aline, Annie's divorced mother, and their daughter, Janie, Annie's half sister, lived in a four-story townhouse on East Twenty-Fourth Street, between Fifth Avenue and University Place. Aline gave small dinner parties with gourmet food and, most impressively, two maids who wore attractive uniforms and white gloves while serving. Talk centered on politics, theater, art, and books. Coincidentally, her closest friend was also named Aline. Aline Bernstein was a well-known theatrical designer, known in the gossip columns as Thomas Wolfe's Jewish mistress. How could that beautiful, talented, educated woman permit Wolfe to abuse her as badly as he did? How could she put up with his boorish behavior? It is admirably explained in her novel, *The Journey Down*, a sad, oh so sad, but beautifully written novel.

Hayes also had a grand country home in Long Island's Sands Point with some two hundred feet of beachfront. Arthur was never idle and had little time for small talk. He was either telephoning, reading, or playing paddle-ball with a neighbor.

My First Wife: The Glamorous Anna Fleisher Friede

Arthur had no patience with Annie's political opinions and that too was a problem; it was bad enough I had no college degree, but I had to take politics on too. What the hell was I doing there? However, on several occasions, a teacher of Communism came to "our" Charles Street apartment to conduct a class. At the time, I was impressed by the concept "From Each According to His Ability, to Each According to His Need." It all seemed so sensible, but that's not the way it worked out. I was never politically active, never solicited funds, never suggested that anyone become active, and never joined Annie at any of the meetings she attended. If Annie ever joined the Party, I never knew it, but she was certainly a very strong believer. Aline and Annie were liberal activists and far to the left. Arthur was one of the founders of the American Civil Liberties Union, militantly backing freedom of speech for the radical right, the Christian Fronters and their followers, even going along with their calls for violence. Annie, her mother, and her stepfather were three strong personalities; conversation at mealtime could be quite heated.

At one of our Sands Point weekends, Billy Rose, an important client, was also a guest. Billy was referred to in the press as the pint-sized impresario, a successful producer of extravaganzas. He was also the owner of the Diamond Horseshoe, New York's first dinner cabaret in the new Paramount Hotel. Add to that his shows at the 1939 New York World's Fair and his blockbuster musical, *Jumbo*, which played at New York's famous Hippodrome. Jumbo was a huge live elephant, the musical's hero. There was always considerable tension when Jumbo was on the stage. What would happen if Jumbo took such a moment to unload? "Little Girl Blue" was the hit song, a standard that continues to be popular.

Billy was a houseguest again on another weekend. At that time he was estranged from his mistress, the swimming star Eleanor Holm. Sunday morning, Aline was taking Billy to a polo match. No one else was going. After breakfast, Aline came out of her bedroom looking every inch the grand dame. She was a handsome woman who knew how to wear clothes. In contrast, Billy was wearing a pair of dark, wrinkled, woolen trousers, a cotton shirt with half sleeves, suspenders, and a straw hat.

Billy suffered from city pallor, a characteristic of people in show business who work at night and sleep all day. They made an incongruous couple, this attractive lady and this short, thin, unattractive man, a product of New York's Lower East Side melting pot. At that time, Billy was very much in the news, involved in a scandal over Milton Berle's girlfriend, a Ziegfeld Follies showgirl.

On a different weekend we were all gathered together after dinner in Arthur's spacious screened-in porch. Roger Baldwin, the founder and executive director of the American Civil Liberties Union, was also a weekend guest. The talk was, what else? Politics. Roger sat at the table reading a book that he was reviewing for *The Sunday Times*. He would read two full pages in the time it would take me to read a paragraph while at the same time participating in the discussion. Roger was well known for his literary efforts. He was also known for having started "his" nude beach on Martha's Vineyard. Watching Baldwin that night gave me a close-up look at the extent to which a fine mind could be stretched.

After our marriage, we moved to a larger apartment; a third-floor walk-up at 685 Hudson Street. There was a den, living room, dining room, kitchen, and bedroom. Much of the furniture was from Annie's Charles Street apartment. We bought whatever else was needed - not much, to be sure. Annie was employed as an assistant designer with Anne Klein and I was still with Ameritex. For our first dinner party, Annie invited a few of her friends. In the middle of dinner there was a phone call from London; it was John Gunther. John was a best-selling author, well known for his series of *Inside* books: *Inside Moscow, Inside Paris, Inside London*, etc. He was moving back to the States and wanted to pick up where they had left off. Annie kept saying, "But John, I'm married. John, I'm married." Gunther, like Max, refused to take no for an answer.

After dinner, and this is so unlike me, I fell asleep. Looking back, it probably was the result of those endless political discussions that seldom resolved anything. I had not yet acquired the skill of directing conversations so that no guest would ever be bored, including me, as host.

The following day, a Sunday in August of 1939, we were puttering around the apartment. As the French say, I am *maladroite*. (In 1945, I learned some conversational French at Berlitz.) I can do nothing with my hands. I was determined, however, that as a married man, I would personally install my own tie rack. It involved putting in two screws. Despite my best efforts, I messed it up and remember blushing with shame and frustration. I didn't realize I lacked the proper tools. We turned the radio on just in time to hear Edward R. Morrow from London. He came out with that all-time shocker: Russia's Communist dictator, Stalin, was joining forces with Hitler and the Nazis. Annie tried to make excuses but there was no way I could accept them, and that day, "From Each According to His Ability, to Each According to His Need" passed into history, at least for me.

Annie was well on her way to becoming a designer. She drew beautiful sketches and shopped the market for new ideas. As a salesman, my future was modest or questionable. Nevertheless, it was a risk that never seemed to bother Annie. I had been a relatively successful salesman. I joined Ameritex in 1936, the year Annie and I were married. It should have been a new start, but I was still not motivated and still came to the office late. I could not take what I did as a salesman seriously.

The status of my new life prompted me to take a good look at myself. Somewhere in my late teens or early twenties, I had come to believe, no, I just knew that I was not destined to live and die in Brooklyn with the people I had known. It was therefore clear that by now I would have become somebody. Yet at twenty-nine I was still, in my own eyes, a nothing –a nobody. If I was ever going to be what I dreamed of, when would that happen? Indeed, if not now, when? Realizing, finally, that I was drifting, that I had been drifting all these many years, I wondered if there wasn't something I could do, or should do, maybe on my own. And at that point, my thoughts turned to Mermelstein.

Dear, dear Mermelstein. I can still see your drawn pale face and reddish hair. Little did you know the change you would make in my life. You were indirectly responsible for the decision to go into business for myself; I would open up a Custom Shop.

5

I Open My First Custom Shop

I have a skinny neck. Although this bit of anatomical news might not strike the reader as earth-shattering, it was in fact, a skinny neck that indirectly launched my career as a shirt maker. I wore a size fifteen collar, but the shirt was too tight in the chest and the shoulders. A fifteen-and-a-half would fit properly through the chest and shoulders, but would be too big in the neck. In 1935, when Mermelstein came into my life, I was still a salesman at Everfast. When I moved to Ameritex, I continued that relation-ship. Mermelstein's father, a refugee from Czarist Russia, had a tiny business making shirts to order from the customer's own material, and I was still one of his regulars. He charged $1.25 for "cut, make, and trim" (buttons, interlining, stays, and pressing). His shirts were produced in a small loft on the Lower East Side. He and his father employed about nine sewing-machine operators. Mermelstein ran the work rooms and his son did the selling by making rounds of the various cotton goods houses, taking shirt orders from employees who wanted shirts made to order from their own material.

Worth Street, in lower Manhattan, had become a center for converters. It was their business to "convert" raw fabric into finished fabrics, silks, and of course, cottons. The converters sold their wares to the manufacturers of shirts, dresses, ladies' sportswear, children's dress, and so on. The manufacturers bought cuttings so they could make samples that would determine which of the sample fabrics they would buy in bulk.

Happily for Mermelstein, sample cuttings frequently found their way into the hands of employees like me. That modest bit of chicanery, commonplace to the trade in those pre-computer days, served as the raison d'être for Mermelstein's business. He would also make pajamas and ladies' shirts from the customer's own material.

In 1937, "upstairs" shirtmakers charged six dollars for shirts custom-made with domestic cotton and as high as fifteen dollars (about $250 today) for Sea Island cotton, the very best. One eventful day in April 1937, I made a calculation on my fingers. If Mermelstein charged $1.25 for "cut, make, and trim," his total cost (labor, rent, trim, buttons, and overhead) was probably seventy-five cents. It took three yards to make a shirt, and in those days the wholesale price for domestic shirtings was eighteen cents a yard. It seemed to me that I could make a shirt for about $1.30 (fifty-four cents for material plus seventy-five cents for labor and overhead) and retail it at two dollars. Arrow shirts were $1.85, and my shirts would be made to order at almost the same price, with a minimal inventory risk.

My idea of selling made-to-order shirts at less than half the price of the "upstairs" shirtmakers seemed almost too good to be true, and the more I thought about it, the more excited I became. This was a fabulous idea that couldn't miss. I was not a shirtmaker and I had never worked in a retail store, nor had I ever been inside a shirt factory, but I knew, intuitively, that with my sense of fashion, I could do better than Mermelstein, a Lower East Side "blue-collar" immigrant.

My thinking on the subject of made-to-order shirts gradually transformed itself into reality. All shirtmakers bought their shirtings from jobbers, middlemen who bought their shirtings from the mills at wholesale prices. The jobbers would sell cuts of fifteen or thirty yards (even three yards), depending on a shirtmaker's needs, at retail prices. I decided to take a calculated risk and go directly to the fabric mills to place orders for full pieces, which was much more than I needed, but I could then buy my shirtings at wholesale.

The mills gave me a hard time, wanting me to buy from jobbers, their customers. I explained that although I was opening only one store and one factory, it was my intention to open thirty-five stores, the first store being only a pilot. If the basic idea was sound, there would be a Custom Shop in every major city, and a city like New York could support five Custom Shops. I finally persuaded the financial officer at one mill to sell me shirtings at mill-level prices. Thus, I was able to create an immediate savings of forty percent on the fabric cost, giving me a further competitive edge, one that was denied the "upstairs" shirtmakers, since they were obliged to buy from jobbers at retailer's prices.

I would hold customers to a minimum order of three shirts, which quickly changed to four. This would lower cutting and administrative costs. It would also increase my start-up volume. Custom Shop would be strictly cash and carry, with no credit losses.

As I quickly learned, to be cost efficient my assembly line demanded a minimum of 1,100 shirts a week. Several Custom Shops would easily give me the necessary volume. Until then, I would limp ahead as best I could. I could easily afford to open stores in prime areas because my rent would always be low since I needed only minimal space with no inventory. Upstairs shirtmakers had a workroom on the premises. My workrooms would be in a low-rent loft, one that would serve all of my branches.

I would open my own factory right from the beginning, thereby saving a contractor's profit. That savings would also be passed on to my customers. Equally exciting, I would be operating in large measure with my customers' money, as I would cut nothing without a substantial deposit. And there was absolutely no doubt in my mind that I could learn Mermelstein's process and improve upon it, even though I had no idea at the time what his system was or exactly how I would do it better. I just <u>knew</u> I could.

I was so excited with my new idea that I thought I would discuss it with my tailor, Mervin Levine. Mervin was doing something similar, making individual suits to order in his factory. He had no store, a low-rent loft, and modest but very successful ads in *The New York Times*.

I said, "Mervin, I can do made-to-order shirts at $2 a piece." He said, "No way, the customers won't believe they're any good. You must charge at least $2.50." I didn't believe him, but I compromised at $2.15.

I talked about the idea with Annie, her father, and her stepfather. Despite my enthusiasm, their response was decidedly negative. They were united in thinking that I did not have what it takes to be a businessman.

I Open My First Custom Shop

At the end of May in 1937, despite all the negative opinions, I decided to resign from Ameritex and start my own business. Was it possible that my secretly held high opinion of myself, that I was not destined to live and die in Brooklyn, was finally to be justified? I walked into Mr. Rossman's office, planning to tell him I intended to start my own business. But before I could get it out, he told me, quite gently, that my services would no longer be required. Once again, my immature performance had caught up with me. I flunked out of high school and had now been fired from four jobs, not exactly an ideal background for starting a new business.

My entire savings were invested in common stocks. In June of 1937, my stocks were worth about $10,000, but I needed to spend no money on my venture until the end of August. One week before I needed cash, the stock market crashed, reducing my heavily margined account from $10,000 to $1,000 overnight.

Disaster. What to do? I borrowed $1,000 on my life insurance policy and with the resulting $2,000, opened my first tiny Custom Shop and a small factory fully stocked with nine rented sewing machines and a respectable inventory of shirt fabrics, collar linings, buttons, boxes, and order forms. My first store opened on the twenty-seventh of September in 1937 and was located at 1370 Broadway and Thirty-Sixth Street, one block up from Macy's. It was one of New York's better shopping blocks, in the garment center, crowded with fashion-conscious men.

I needed a unique storefront because my store was only seven feet wide and my window only two feet wide. Fortunately, it was four feet deep, and it fanned out in back from twenty-four to thirty-eight inches. That first storefront was made of black Carrara glass; a red-and-white-striped dome awning called attention to my little window. That awning became my logo and eventually was better known than the Custom Shop name.

I was sure my new business would be successful but so fearful that my "fabulous idea" would be immediately copied, that I actually kept it a secret from the real estate agent who rented me that first store. Nor did I tell the men who applied for the foreman's job exactly what I was doing either (I had placed a classified ad in *The New York Times*). I told each applicant just enough to decide he could do the job. When I finally decided on the man I wanted, I took him into my complete confidence. He had to show me how to take measurements. Since he had very little experience in custom-made shirts and I had none at all, it was another case of the blind leading the blind. Don't laugh yet, because that's only the beginning. I was lucky that Jack Keenan, who worked part-time for Mermelstein as a cutter, came to me with his much-needed know-how.

The night prior to the opening, Annie sent me home at midnight, saying that I had to get some sleep if I was to open the next morning. She stayed on with the window trimmer to complete whatever had to be done. I dreamed that my opening was so successful I had to call out the mounted police to keep people in line. So I was on a high when I opened my door the next morning. The window looked good, and a hand-lettered sign told my story:

Our Story Is a Simple One

We have devised a method whereby, we can afford to custom make shirts to your individual measurements with collar styles designed to complement your particular neck and face, at $2.15, provided three or more shirts are ordered.

I was so very proud of that copy. Hard to believe it came from me, because until then, I had written nothing more than an occasional "Wish you were here" postcard. But, and please pay attention to this, that thrilling piece of copy betrayed me, and put a taint on my company's reputation, which stands to this day. An inexperienced schlemiel can make big mistakes without knowing it.

That one line, "We have devised a method…" permitted journalists and salesmen at other stores to speculate about our methods. There was no way to stop their theorizing and that is how a myth developed that our shirts were not custom made, not even made to measure. The truth is that the fit of my shirts was better on average than the fit of other shirtmakers because we gave customers a fitting *before* we cut their shirts. I conceived the idea of using a shell to determine the configuration and that was a terrific improvement. A tape can measure the body, but it cannot measure the configuration, the shape of the body, nor can it measure the customer's mind; who wants his shirts loose, or who wants his shirt fitted. With a shell (a collar-less, half-sleeve shirt in his chest size), the customer can show the shirtmaker the exact looseness, the exact fit he prefers.

At ten minutes to nine, I had just finished sweeping the floor when a man knocked on the door. I was hit with an acute attack of stage fright. I said, "Sorry sir, we're not open yet, please come back at nine-thirty." Two minutes later, another man tried to open the door. I realized then that if I was actually going to be in business, I had no choice; I was forced to admit customers. I opened the door, put away my broom, and turned on the lights.

Mr. Austin selected three shirts, and I took his measurements. I was so green, not realizing what I didn't know. My beginnings were indeed primitive: there were just six shirts hanging on the wall with six different collar styles. When Austin selected the collar style he wanted, I realized that I had failed to identify the styles with names or pattern numbers. So, in the space indicated for collar style, I had to write, "Third collar from right on the wall."

At the close of business that day, I removed the six shirts from the wall and took them to my Twenty-eighth Street factory along with the orders. Since I had neglected to keep the shirts in sequence, my improvised instructions became meaningless. Can you believe it? No, you can't, but that was indeed the beginning.

My first order for three shirts totaled $6.45, plus thirteen cents sales tax (a blessedly low two percent). I had decided to cut no shirt without a twenty-five percent deposit, so I proceeded to multiply $6.58 by twenty-five percent (no calculators). In my confused state, it was beyond my ability, and I might still find it difficult. Blushing furiously, I said, "Perhaps you can give me a three-dollar deposit." (The simplifier.)

The customer said, "Fine," and handed me a ten-dollar bill. I hadn't known either, that a retailer starts his day with cash in the drawer for making change. Actually, I had neither a cash drawer nor change. I suggested that he go to the cigar store in the lobby and get his bill changed. By then, my customer must surely have had some misgivings. Nevertheless he came back and gave me the $3. Despite this rather ludicrous beginning, customers kept coming in. They came in off the street, attracted by the window display and by the extraordinarily low price.

Now, I knew that the quality of my shirts would not be what they should be in the beginning, and they weren't. It is not possible to start a new factory and get top quality. However, I knew that the fit would be much, much better than my customer could get in a ready-made shirt and, of course, it was. I also knew that New York   was a big city, and the supply of new customers would be steady, even while all the bugs were being ironed out. New customers kept coming in and, as predicted, the shirts did get better. However, one disastrous day is still painfully etched in my memory.

I vividly recall an afternoon some two months after I opened; there were six customers in my tiny store; it was filled to capacity. Two men wanted to order shirts and were looking at the shirtings. Two other men were complaining. "You said the shirts would be here by three o'clock and I need them, now!" Another man was saying, "These shirts were promised last week and they're still not here." A fifth man was saying, "Is this the way you think a custom shirt should fit?" (The sleeves were too long.) And the sixth man was pointing out that his shirts fit fine but he knew he never ordered a button-down collar, because he wouldn't be caught dead in a button-down collar.

Annie came by at 6:00 to find me thoroughly discouraged, not to the point of giving up, but depressed by realizing how little I knew and how much there was to learn. For the first time in my grown-up life I was in despair. I was sitting on a low stool, Annie was standing. She put her arm around me, and I rested my head on her bosom and let myself be consoled. I certainly needed it. It has been said that big trees from little acorns grow, but it would be surprising if anything other than ulcers could grow from the problems of starting a new business by someone so hopelessly unprepared.

Happily, my start-up problems were partially resolved, and for this I have to thank Andrew Seligson, at least in part. I had been in business for two months when Seligson walked in, a vision out of *Esquire* magazine. He was wearing a bowler hat, a black Chesterfield coat with a velvet collar, a starched white shirt collar, a handsome black tie with small white polka-dots, yellow chamois gloves, and a furled umbrella. He was about thirty-five, short, dapper, and looked as though he could take on the world. He asked,

"Are you the proprietor?"

"Yes."

"This is an interesting idea you have here. My name is Andrew Seligson. I was in charge of the custom shirt department at Saks Fifth Avenue, and am presently in charge of the custom shirt department at Freems of the Waldorf." Freems was one of New York's most expensive clothing stores, located in Park Avenue's Waldorf-Astoria hotel. "If you would like a partner, I'd be interested, and I know everything there is to know about the custom shirt business."

I said, "Unfortunately, I know practically nothing about the custom shirt business, but I really don't want a partner."

"Perhaps we can work something out."

"Perhaps we can. I intend to open thirty-five stores. We can form a partnership, but only for store number two – no part of store number one or my workrooms."

Seligson said, "That would be okay. Let me work with you for the next two months. I'll work for nothing, let's say $25 a week, and if this is as good as it looks, we'll draw up a contract."

"Good."

Although I had been learning fast, it's fair to say that Seligson took over immediately. Actually, he looked brighter than he turned out to be. At the end of two months, he brought in an accountant. Together they told me I was bankrupt. Seligson's accountant said my business needed $10,000 in additional capital. Seligson's proposal was that he would put up $5,000, I would put up

$5,000, and we would then be fifty-fifty partners in the entire business, including my factory and existing store.

I said, "But Andrew, that wouldn't be at all equitable. You will put up $5,000, but only for a half-interest in the second store. It's my idea, it's my business, and I'm not bankrupt."

Seligson said, "Mortimer, your concept is great but you haven't the foggiest idea of what you're doing. You can't possibly continue without my expertise or without additional capital. If we don't make a deal, I'll set up a competitive business; you'll never survive."

Seligson's accountant had calculated that the customers' deposits were a liability, since the deposits were money I owed them until I delivered the shirts. From an accounting point of view, he was right. But as a pragmatic neophyte, I knew he was wrong because all those sales would be concluded profitably, as they were.

My father-in-law said, "Mortimer, you are not a businessman. I'll lend you the $5,000. Take Seligson in." I was almost in tears.

"It's not equitable," I said, "and I can't do it. I don't need the $5,000, but thanks anyway."

Because Seligson was greedy, he lost a chance to buy half of Custom Shop for $10,000. It would have earned him millions. I turned down his offer because it wasn't a fair deal. He was arrogant and, as it turned out, stupid. The profits continued, and they were all mine. I continued as founder and sole owner for the next sixty years.

So Seligson walked out, saying, "Mortimer, you'll rue the day." I borrowed no money from my father-in-law or anyone else, not then and not ever, and three years later opened my ninth store, this one in Philadelphia. There, I inadvertently learned that Seligson was managing a small ladies' hosiery shop on Chestnut Street. I never heard from him again. Of such decisions are fortunes made and lost.

I Open My First Custom Shop

Considering my ridiculously shaky start, it might be reasonable to think that "somebody" was in my corner. Yet you should not conclude that my subsequent success was merely due to heavenly intervention or even luck. I was well financed because every customer had to give me a fifty percent deposit. However, I was not really qualified to start my Custom Shop because I was not a shirtmaker, not a retailer, and lacked any experience in business or administration.

Nevertheless, I contributed many innovative concepts that were totally different from the way things had been done in the past. And those new concepts were, in large part, responsible for maintaining Custom Shop's unique success. As I write this last line I wondered what would have happened to me, what would my life have been like if I hadn't met Mermelstein, and if his business hadn't triggered my concept for Custom Shop. Would I have continued to be a nothing? It's an interesting question because there is no answer – or is there?

6

Elements of My

Astonishing Success

Perhaps I should explain why I was so wildly successful. Fifty-one years after its inadequate opening, Custom Shop had eighty-two stores from coast to coast. No partners, no stockholders, no franchise, no debt, and believe it or not, not a single competitive chain. On two separate occasions, my own executives secured financing to open competitive chains. The Shirt Gallery succeeded in opening thirty-one stores before filing for bankruptcy. And a competitor in Washington, I don't remember the name of the company, but the name was very British. They opened fourteen stores before going broke.

Saks Fifth Avenue and various other retailers charged fifty percent more for an identical quality shirt because their shirts were all made by a contractor, adding the contractor's profit to the cost. That extra cost was then passed on to the customer who also had to pay for the additional mark-up on the extra cost. A retailer who charges fifty percent more for a similar quality is not a real competitor.

Actually, I opened up my own competition long before any of the others. And here's how that came about. Irwin Friedlander (Friedy), Custom Shop's second executive vice president, had resigned in 1942, to be replaced by Harry Harris. Subsequently, in 1947, I returned from a six-month European holiday to discover that Friedy had opened up his own store, called deFries. It was a more luxurious store than any Custom Shop I had at that time. DeFries had a corner location on Madison Avenue and Fifty-Fifth Street. Custom Shop never had a corner location. I bought deFries from Friedy as the basis for a competitive upscale chain, and brought Friedy back as president.

Friedy carried only ready-mades because he was too smart to compete with custom-made. I installed custom-made shirts at deFries. DeFries would charge $1 more per shirt than Custom Shop –a small price to pay for the luxury of ordering custom-made shirts from deFries. Theoretically, deFries would catch customers who had been disappointed at Custom Shop, or customers who were happy with Custom Shop but thought they were ready to take one step up.

We had a successful first year and then watched the custom shirt business go down in 1948 and 1949. In 1950, I changed the name from deFries to Custom Shop and sales shot up immediately. So I knew, way back then, that a successful competitive chain would be unlikely. Custom Shop shirtmakers had really arrived.

There are a variety of reasons why a man might want to have a shirt custom-made:

·He has my problem: collar-size, 15, and body size, 15 1/2, or vice versa.

·He has a favorite collar style that is no longer in fashion.

·He has a favorite fabric that he can't find in ready-made shirts.

·His arms are extra long or extra short or one arm is longer than the other, so he can't get the proper sleeve length in ready-made shirts.

·Because of his height, he needs a tail length different than he can find in a ready-made shirt.

·He wants a snug fit, or an oversize fit.

·He wants to design his own collar style.

·He needs a "quarter-size" collar (16 is too tight, 16 1/2 is too large, so he needs 16 1/4).

·He wants French cuffs on an Oxford button-down, or a two-button cuff rather than a one-button cuff. He wants an Oxford shirt without a button-down collar.

·He likes the idea of having shirts custom-made.

·He likes to drop names like "my shirtmaker." For many, it's prestigious.

Custom Shop was highly recommended, and that's not all.

Primarily, Custom Shop's success stemmed from my realization that the only extra money required for a custom-made shirt was the relatively modest extra cost of cutting a shirt individually versus cutting them in bulk, plus the extra time required to take measurements and write up an order, which in most cases runs about an hour.

The thirty minutes of a designer's time, compared to the fifteen minutes it takes a salesclerk to sell a ready-made shirt, was compensated for by prices based on cutting three shirts (now four) rather than one. The extra cost was partially covered by the fact that I was the maker, by-passing the manufacturer's profit. Too simple? Not at all. I was indeed a manufacturer, selling directly to the consumer through my own stores. This made it possible for our custom-made shirts to be priced almost the same as ready-made shirts of comparable quality.

Perhaps I should explain what was meant by the line "We have devised a method" in my window copy. Obviously, it costs more to cut shirts individually than it does to cut ready-made shirts that are piled one hundred high and then cut completely by machine. However, once the shirts are individually cut to the measurements taken by our designers, the big savings start. I "devised a method" whereby, after the shirts are cut, they can then be sewn on an assembly line system, just like ready-made shirts, giving my customers the kind of savings Henry Ford created when he developed his assembly line.

I processed the thirty-one separate operations in the sewing of a shirt with a similar assembly line concept. That's why I needed minimum sales of 1,100 shirts a week for a cost-efficient operation. "Upstairs" shirtmakers use one operator to sew the entire shirt, a setup that requires an extremely skilled operator. Such a person was hard to find then and continues to be just as hard to find. More important, it costs twice as much. That process is also more costly because it takes much more time to sew. On the other hand, our operators develop even greater skill because each of them does only one operation. The key to getting quality in our system is having the proper number of inspections as the shirt moves down the line. Inspectors must make sure that each operation is done precisely.

That the system paid off is seen by the fact that only two and a half percent of our shirts required an alteration because of a fit problem. Some of these were due only to errors in writing down or reading the original order. This in itself seems a minor miracle, taking into account that there are thirteen individual measurements (four on the collar and nine on the body) that must be taken correctly and written correctly, along with seven-digit fabric numbers.

Is image important? Of course it is. Remove a general's uniform and you have an old man with erect posture. Remove Toscanini's "white tie uniform," the one he wears when conducting, and you have a short, old man with white hair. Truman needed his hat to project some semblance of a president. When he appeared on television in his Hawaiian flowered shirt, his stature was diminished to the original role he played as the partner in a small men's store in Kansas City.

In fact, image was so important to IBM that Tom Watson, Jr., the man who made IBM so enormously successful, was also known for one particular memo that stated, in effect, "Our customers are businessmen, we should dress like businessmen." Years later, when the company was floundering, IBM's new chairman, Lou Gerstner, also thought that image was important. He started his tenure with a memo that stated, in effect, "I know what's wrong with IBM. IBM is too stuffy and we are going casual." Not just dress-down Friday, but dress-down everyday. Gerstner failed to get the look he expected, as evidenced by this message from headquarters:

A man should look as good as he is—even better if possible.

Collection of the author

From: Michael J. Murphy

Director of Operations, CHQ Armonk (Corporate Headquarters)

Date: 07/29/96

Subject: Dress Code

As you know, we have evolved to a less formal dress standard in IBM, including here at Armonk. Overall, we use good judgment in determining when "business casual dress" is and isn't appropriate.

Elements of My Astonishing Success

You are probably waiting for the "however" in this letter, so here it is. There have been instances where some of us have not used good judgment in this area . . . and have not kept in mind the principles that should guide us. These principles are:

Dress for the customer.

Use common sense.

Remember: This is headquarters, and we frequently host customers. Jeans, t-shirts, and sneakers, for example, are not appropriate for this environment.

All this will be particularly important in our new building, which will feature an open workspace plan and where we expect an increase in customer visits. So let's enjoy the comfort of business casual but keep the customer in mind.

Thanks for you help with this.

Lou Gerstner's well-meant memo helped put three thousand clothing stores out of business across the nation. Gerstner assumed that his executives would know how to dress casually for business. Sneakers, t-shirts, and shorts revealed only too clearly the depth of their ignorance in this area. That ignorance was not confined to IBM. Six months of the year I used to spend Saturday afternoons in my flagship store, located in Rockefeller Center at 716 Fifth Avenue, directly opposite Saks. I sat in a comfortable chair and watched the operation on the second floor, where customers come to order custom-made shirts and custom-made suits. Every Saturday I wondered how all those blue-collar workers could afford to order custom-made clothes.

One afternoon I asked to see the cards attached to the back of the orders. The results were startling. Those customers only looked blue collar in their casual clothes, yet they were mostly executives: presidents, CEOs, lawyers, doctors, television executives, theatrical producers, and even actors. What they all had in common was a lack of education in the subject of image.

Most men continue to suffer from the trauma induced by mothers when they were little boys. And that trauma is relived when wives, who really care about image, begin nagging. "When are you going to get a haircut? Your suits never look right, neither does your shirt collar, and it's time you got some new neckties."

Men look their very best in evening clothes, the tuxedo: plain black suit, plain white shirt, plain black tie. Ah, and there's the twist; if the black tie was a normal four in hand, he would be dressed for a funeral. It's the bow-tie that makes the difference. Men look better in formal clothes and in military uniforms because both were designed by professional designers to bypass personal taste.

The casual look has been put into the hands of men who have no taste of their own, and the subject of image has never been part of the curriculum in high school or in college. The result has lowered the male image to a level equaled by the Russians during the height of the Cold War but below the Chinese male image. For the most part, Chinese men looked well put together in their Mao suits. Frankly, the casual look does not project the affluent image of the American male.

To measure the distance of their deterioration, one need only look at the image projected by men in the *Upstairs/Downstairs* television series; the time period from 1900 to 1929. God, they were elegant, even the servants.

The destruction of image is widespread. Nurses used to look like professionals dressed in crisp white poplin, topped by a white mini-hat. That professional look increased patient confidence. Today's nurses, at least those in the New York Hospital, come dressed in the clothes they wear in the subway. One cannot differentiate between nurses and staff. Nurses with make-up hastily applied, hair put together in a hurry, clothes frequently wrinkled and even soiled. This is the unfortunate result of a nurse's union vote that failed to understand the importance of a professional image.

It's interesting to see that the current look for executives calls for chinos, the kind of trousers that have been standard for janitors in corporate buildings, although their chinos are sometimes gray.

Elements of My Astonishing Success

If these pages had been written by Tom Wolfe, the reader might better have understood the sloppy look I am describing. But to really understand it, there is no alternative to actually seeing these "blue-collar executives" who were ordering custom-made shirts and suits those Saturday afternoons.

I took time out one day to visit Ralph Lauren's flagship store on Madison Avenue and Seventy-Second Street, the six-story mansion that he converted into a showplace for his various products: shirts, ties, suits, sport jackets, slacks, casual wear, sheets, bed covers, towels, and antiques. I had not been there since it first opened. Lauren had advertised in *The Sunday Times Magazine*; a handsome tweed suit that I wanted to try on. If it looked as good as I thought, I would get the fabric and have it custom made.

That store was so beautiful –it was breathtaking. Lauren paid no attention to cost; this was his legacy. Wherever I looked, every corner reflected this man's taste, and I thought Ralph really is an artist. Jackson Pollock, de Kooning, and Rothko, for example, pale by comparison. I was thrilled, really thrilled. I know, because the hair was standing up on the back of my neck. However I was totally unprepared for the customers (gobs of customers), whose lack of taste and lack of understanding defiled the ambiance. If it were possible, most of them should have been barred at the entrance. Their presence was a desecration. It was another case of "pearls before swine."

The importance of image is plain to see and the value of an attractive image is sometimes self-evident. I had been lunching occasionally at "21" with Bob Batscha, president of the Museum of Television and Radio (Sadly, Bob died at the early age of fifty-eight on July 4, 2003). The head waiter evidently recognized me and on my last visit, said, "Mr. Levitt, this is my twenty-third year here, and you are, in my opinion, the best-dressed customer we've ever had." To get that posy at my age is indeed unexpected.

Think of "image" as one of the advantages of civilized living. Think of "dressing up" as having fun by adding to your individuality like good food, good wine, good books, good theater, and other sources of pleasure. The importance of image began in the Garden of Eden, with one fig leaf for Eve and two fig leaves for Adam. The concept was quickly picked up by the Aborigines who painted their black bodies with white stripes. There followed a long list of improvements in image that crested in French vulgarity. The white powdered wigs for men, and the merciless application of makeup; faces that were heavily painted white, heavily rouged with too much make-up around the eyes. I believe the male image peaked in England with English aristocracy in the period just before the First World War.

Indeed, image helped England build its empire. London's famous Changing of the Guard performance was a prototype for the many similar shows they put on in India and their other colonies. The English image, spearheaded by the royalty of a King or Queen, spelled out by unchallengeable power.

Your face is always up front, I repeat, always up front. And your shirt collar is important, because, like the setting for your wife's diamond ring, the collar acts as a setting for your face. You will not understand its importance until you see the improvement in image that takes place when the collar is custom made and designed by a shirtmaker who understands his craft.

A necktie completes the collar. Based upon our experience, nine men out of ten do not know how to knot a tie properly. Is Image Important? Of course it is, second only to substance.

7

Our Tricky Divorce

After two and a half years Annie and I threw in the towel. It was 1939. There were no serious incidents, there were no quarrels about money, and there were no children. The marriage just didn't work. That first night I moved into the Hotel Russell on Park Avenue at Thirty-Seventh Street. They had no rooms, only a suite, but as it was late, they gave me a suite for the price of a room. But for me, the suite was no bargain. A suite is desirable for someone who might need to entertain. I was alone, and the suite brought my aloneness into sharp perspective. The thing I missed most that night was our paintings and that came as an unlikely surprise. Our paintings helped convert our apartment into a home. I had never realized how much the paintings mattered until I was confronted with the innocuous pictures hanging on the hotel walls. I already missed our home.

We agreed to a divorce. In those days the only grounds for divorce was adultery. We had a choice: a quick trip to Mexico, even though Mexican divorces were not legally recognized, or a six-week stay in Reno, which was out of the question because of my new business. So now it was a question of who sues who. Does Annie go to court and accuse me or do I go to court and accuse Annie? Going to court and blatantly lying in public would be unpleasant for either of us. I was elected to do the dirty work. Our lawyer did all the things that were required. I went to court, the decree was issued, and the marriage was dissolved. We were divorced and there was no question of alimony.

We remained friends. After I remarried, Annie was a frequent guest at our home and we were frequent guests at hers. Her third husband, Allan Shore, was also a political activist. They subsequently divorced, remarried, and divorced again. In 1973 she was living alone in the West 70s –a charming duplex in a brownstone.

One night when Mimi and I were at her house for dinner, Annie told us that even though she had to take a cut in pay, she was giving up her job to become director of personnel at a union and would be moving to a less expensive apartment. The next day I phoned her and said, "Annie, you can't give up that apartment, it's too lovely. I will send you a check every month for the difference in rent. You must stay there." She said, "I can't take your money, you have no reason to do it." I said, "Don't be stupid, it's a matter of aesthetics." I started sending the checks immediately so that she wouldn't have to move. Annie refused my offer by sending the checks back.

Several years later, however, she did ask if I would consider giving her a mortgage on a brownstone she wanted to buy on Boerum Hill, in Brooklyn. And of course, I did it with pleasure. She made her payments on time and when she died, she owed me nothing. Annie taught me a lot, yet one day she confessed that I had been her "best husband."

Maybe there are happy bachelors, but I was not one. As men before me have undoubtedly discovered, money does not obliterate loneliness. Nor does money buy happiness. Shortly after the divorce, Walter Desauer, my eccentric German-born friend, suggested a trip to Bermuda. We were to go by boat (two days each way), and for me that would be a new experience. Walter was handsome and blue-eyed, projecting the typical blonde-haired image of a WASP. But, to use a well-worn cliché, you can't judge a book by its cover. Walter was a German Jewish refugees who had escaped Hitler's net.

In 1939, most of Bermuda's hotels were restricted – "No Jews." Poor Walter. The Christian girls on the boat, of course, took him to be one of their own. With anti-Semitism a given, Walter had to continue "passing" if he wanted to make any headway. We didn't try to get a hotel reservation, but settled for a bed and breakfast.

We spent our days at Coral Beach which was beautiful beyond any beach I'd ever seen, so unlike the coarse tan sand and murky water on Coney Island, or the private Manhattan Beach with its admission charge. The sand at Coral Beach was white, clean, dry, and silky. The water was crystal clear. It was nature showing off. The focal point of our existence, however, was girls and for us they were nonexistent except for the one night when Walter, having made contact, took a girl out to dinner.

In 1939, girls were not as giving as today. After dinner, Walter tried to make love to his lady against a tree. She was very willing up to a point, at which she said, "Sorry, Walter, but that's where I draw the line," and she was not to be dissuaded. The next day, Walter sent her a pad of paper, a pencil, and a ruler, with a note saying, "Drawing lines can be great fun. Enjoy." (*Telephone call – Walter is dead.*)

When we got back to New York, I found a small penthouse apartment at 302 West Twelfth Street with an entrance on Abingdon Square. At that time, my ever-loving Aunt Anna was living with Mother in Brooklyn. I found them an apartment on Central Park West, overlooking the park, a long overdue token of an obligation. And that summer, vacationing at Camp Copake, a camp for adults, I met Betty Lynn. Betty was a dancer, one of five girls who had formed their own group, a self-contained program of modern choreography. Theirs was one of the acts in the regular weekend show. They also taught dancing to guests. Betty was lovely to look at, serious and dedicated to dance. We became lovers.

Betty. A serious dancer of modern ballet.

8

In 1941,

Three Years and Ten Months

From the Beginning, I Retire

In 1937, I needed a man to run my first store; I went to Macy's shirt department to find one. I pretended that I wanted to buy shirts from an attractive salesman, George Zimmerman. After a while, I confessed. I said, "George, I'm opening a new business called Custom Shop. I <u>know</u> it's going to be successful but I do <u>not</u> want to be a businessman. So, in five years I will retire and you will run the business. If you can't handle it then the next guy will. And if he can't, then the guy after that will, but it won't be me."

I was thinking back to the "Boss", the bully who made life miserable for Harry Harris, the office manager, picking on him like picking on a scab. The "Boss" represented, in my mind, what it was like to be an exploiter, and I wanted no part of it. Communism may have been responsible for some of my thinking: the boss as villain. George was enchanted. And believe it or not, that's exactly what happened.

I walked out in three years and ten months, on the thirtieth of June in 1941; one year earlier than promised and George took over. To get myself in good shape for retirement, I went to Bill Brown's physical training farm in Harrison, New York, for a three-week stay. It was interesting for several reasons but especially because it was for men only. There, I discovered that with no women to chase I was completely at peace, not at all restless. It was the first time ever that I had a chance to be in an all-male environment. Bill Brown was New York's former boxing commissioner, and in those days Bill was a big shot and he took a liking to me.

Bill Brown's physical training farm, with a view of the Hudson River, was a refuge for overweight men, alcoholic priests, type-A businessmen, and professionals who in some cases were on the verge of a breakdown. It was a sparse existence, with no smoking, no drinking, low-calorie meals, and exercise-filled mornings with a luxurious massage for a reward. To my surprise, I did not enjoy the alleged luxury of being massaged. Afternoons were free for tennis, golf, and riding horseback.

Joe Louis' Training Camp was just across the Hudson River and Joe was training for his next fight. Joe, in his heyday, was a four-star celebrity, the most famous black male in America, the world's heavyweight champ. In those circles, Bill Brown was a three-star celebrity. Bill took me along for a visit. I had been a Friday night regular for the Madison Square Garden fights and Bill had actually seen me there. Because I was Bill's friend, I too became a celebrity (two stars). Joe was a handsome, friendly man with considerable presence. We talked with him while he was being massaged; it was a great afternoon, this was real backstage. For the first time in my life, I realized that the black community had just as many social levels as the white community. That was evident, seeing so many of the other guests dressed in all their finery. Frankly, it was a revelation giving me new insights – remember this was 1941.

To celebrate my new retirement, I decided to take a six-month trip around the United States. Betty would be free to live in my apartment while I was gone. The idea of the trip was an enormous mistake. How could I have messed up so badly? I overlooked the bottom line: I would be traveling alone.

I bought myself a brand new Chrysler Imperial convertible, at the time, Chrysler's most luxurious car. Back then it was called the New Yorker. I had decided to take the southern route going to California and the northern route coming back. My first stop was in Atlanta where Annie's brother, Wally, was living with his wife, Ziporah. Zippy was a Bennington graduate, an activist, and a dog lover. When I arrived, she was making newspaper headlines. An Atlanta milk processor was selling milk from his plant at wholesale prices in half-gallon containers. The retailers had put up a fuss to prevent the retail sale of milk at wholesale prices. Zippy led the consumer fight to continue buying through the wholesaler. I stayed there just two days and both were focused upon her milk activities. I was surprised to learn that something like this would make front page headlines. Live and learn.

Photo by Ray Levitt
I was thirty-four and retired.

I remember nothing else from that stay other than a visit to a black church service of the Holy Rollers. I had to see it to believe it. The exuberance of the worshipers bordered on hysteria.

Once I crossed the Mississippi, the landscape was endlessly fascinating. The trip climaxed with the drive from Oklahoma City, northwest to Taos, New Mexico. Taos was well known for its Indian reservation, a reservation that welcomed tourists. Taos was even better known as an artists' community. Georgia O'Keefe was at the time its most famous resident. The drive south from Taos to Santa Fe was luscious; there is nothing like it in the east. Most of the time the road bordered a bubbly brook running through a deeply shaded canyon, bursting with semi-tropical plantings. I was, to put it mildly, enchanted.

The Taos drive started the beginning of a devastating internal ache, an emptiness that came with the realization that I was totally alone, that these singular emotional and aesthetic experiences would have to be taken alone. There was no one to share them with. That thought hit me like a punch in the belly. The New Mexico landscape was a revelation. It was an experience I felt with my mind and my whole body.

The trip from Taos to Santa Fe, the hazardous journey down the Grand Canyon and up, the trip through the unbelievable Carlsbad Caverns, and skiing for the first time on CCC (Civilian Conservation Corps) Trails, snow-covered in the Catskill Mountains, head my list of unforgettable experiences.

The trip to the bottom of the Grand Canyon was more than I bargained for. A large percentage of the tourists go down on mules in groups of ten or fifteen. The group goes halfway down, stops for a picnic lunch, before turning around for the trip back to the top. However, I had elected to spend the night in the bottom of the Canyon. The Phantom Ranch, a small inn at the bottom, took care of those few adventurous souls who had the time and the money to go all the way.

I had engaged Toby as my personal guide for the two-day trip. Toby and I joined the group assembling at the top when I overheard one woman saying to her friend, "Oh dear, I'm so frightened." I said, "Excuse me, madam," in my most supercilious tone, "there is nothing to be frightened about. If the trip was dangerous, it would have been stopped long ago or, at the very least, you would have had to sign a paper relieving the company of any responsibility. So, don't worry your pretty head, you're going to enjoy the trip down and enjoy the trip up." Oh my, was I ever wrong.

The Grand Canyon is some five thousand feet deep. The walls are indeed precipitous and the trail to the bottom had to be carved out of those walls. The trails are only about seven or eight feet wide and full of hairpin turns. Fifteen minutes down, the fun began. The guide momentarily stopped us. I happened to be in the middle of a hairpin turn. My mule's four feet were on the ground but his entire neck was sticking out over the precipice, and as far as I was concerned I was sticking out over the precipice too. As they used to say in Brooklyn, "I was scared shitless."

Three Years and Ten Months From the Beginning, I Retire

Unbeknownst to me, I had been hit with vertigo. I did my best to let common sense prevail but the trip down was torture almost every time we made a hairpin turn. There was, however, one consolation. On the way back, the mule's neck would never extend over the edge because we would always be turning into the trail, not away from it.

If there were other guests at the Phantom Ranch that night, I have no recollection. The next morning, my cowboy Toby said, "We're going to see a lovely waterfall." It was located two miles up the river. When we got to the falls we dismounted, Toby built a fire, and we had an early lunch. With the falls serving as our background he said, "Come along now and we can walk under the falls." Sure enough, there was a walking path. The falls were located at the bend in the "U" of a horseshoe-shaped trail, and that was where we could walk under the falls.

I hadn't realized that the trail had been leading up all the time. When we came out from under the falls, we were about a hundred feet up, looking down on nothing but sharp rocks. I was really suffering from vertigo and I was scared. Unfortunately, it didn't end there. The trail took a gentle slope down toward the river. I was paying little attention when suddenly I was surprised to see that the trail was blocked by a huge boulder.

Toby said, "Excuse me," and, grabbing the boulder with both hands and arms, stepped around it to the other side. As I recall, a thirty-inch step over nothing was required. I said, "Hey, Toby there's no way I can make that step." I had looked down on a precipitous fall to jagged rocks. "Toby," I said, "it's not for me." He finally persuaded me to take the step by saying that if I should slip he was strong enough to hold me, so there was no way I could fall. Toby was six-foot-two with broad shoulders and I had reason to believe him. Nevertheless, I was in a cold sweat when I clasped his wrist and he clasped mine.

After lunch we started our climb to the rim. One of the unexpected wonders of the trip down the canyon was the change in climate and vegetation at five thousand feet up. When we assembled at the top, there had been a slight snowfall. When we reached the bottom, we were in the tropics. I looked forward to a safe trip up, to repeat, because we would always be turning in towards the top. It never occurred to me that at one steep hairpin turn the mule's cinch would break. The saddle started to slip back and I could feel myself falling. My life was saved by waking up –a story that climaxes with a dream is cheating, please forgive. I seldom remember dreams, but that dream was a nightmare and has actually repeated itself several times.

The Carlsbad Canyons, three hundred miles to the south, were not on the route. That meant a six-hundred-mile detour. However, I had heard so much about the caverns as a must-see that I decided to leave my car and fly down. I was not at all prepared for what I found. On the side of a gentle grass-covered hill, God or man had carved a symmetrical opening about the size of the oval-shaped stage of Radio City Music Hall. I bought a ticket and walked out of the bright sunshine into the gloom of a cave.

A cave? The room was enormous, as big as Radio City Music Hall, which seats six thousand people. We entered the caverns from what would be, in effect, the last seat in the last row of the third balcony. This huge space was then entered by a long gentle staircase, lit on one side by an endless string of small bulbs about the size of long candlewicks. One gradually walked along one side of the wall, down wooden steps to the bottom. While I am not a believer, this scenic, mysterious masterpiece made me wonder, could there possibly be a God? I decided, once again, no. But how then can one explain this incredible miracle of nature? The bottom of the cave was about one mile long, an enchanted tunnel with beautiful stalactites and even a modest slow moving stream.

Crossing the Rockies was an experience not unlike the experiences I have had crossing New York's Adirondack Mountains on the way to skiing in Canada. The Rockies were bigger but not all that different. However, what lay ahead was Palm Springs, Hollywood's playground in the desert. Back then its social center was Charles Farrell's glamorous Palm Springs Racquet Club. Although I am a teetotaler, I went to a bar the night I arrived. The bar was oval and there sitting on the other side was Ben Oakland, my beloved composer friend who had also left Brooklyn behind and was now well established composing music for the movies.

Benny played the piano by ear and when I was younger, I could listen to him forever. I was his number one fan. I was sixteen when I met Benny and it was miraculous to me that he could play so beautifully, and do it by ear. Even at that early age, Benny was a composer. In 1930 he joined up with two other men: Murray, Trivers, and Oakland became the trio that wrote much of the music for the *Ziegfeld Follies of 1930.* Benny gave me a warm welcome and the next day invited me to lunch at the Racquet Club. He introduced me to Herbert Marshall, the English actor. Marshall's acknowledgment of the introduction was overwhelmingly gracious; how very pleased he was to meet Mr. Levitt. Actually, he made me quite uncomfortable and on further recollection it occurs to me that possibly the man had been drinking. Ben recommended that I stay at the Beverly Hills Hotel in Los Angeles because "that's where the action is."

When Reenie Stein, the beautifully groomed but shy sixteen-year-old girlfriend I had when I was eighteen, heard about my trip to California, she said, "Mortie, you must say hello to Herbert. You remember, my older brother. Herbert writes the gossip column for the *Hollywood Reporter*'s front page and is a man with considerable clout. When you get to Beverly Hills you must look him up." I did. Hearing that I was alone, he said, "Mortimer, I have a lovely girl for you. Her name is Ellis. I know you'll like her and Ellis will like you. I'll tell her to expect your call." I invited Ellis to dinner and she said that would be very nice. I asked where she lived so I could pick her up and she said that wouldn't be necessary, she'd come to the hotel.

To my horror, and I use that word precisely, Ellis turned out to be a call girl. My loneliness deepened. Oh, the irony. A self-made, retired multimillionaire, healthy, reasonably good looking, whose two successful Beverly Hills friends could find for me only a call girl? It was devastating. I was so disappointed, I decided not to take advantage of her professionalism; we had dinner together and I paid her fee.

While I was in Palm Springs, Benny had introduced me to Marsha, Buddy Clark's ex-wife. Buddy Clark was a baritone second only to Bing Crosby. I met Marsha again in Beverly Hills and we enjoyed several pleasant dinners together. She was taking the children to Chicago to spend Christmas with their father who was appearing at Chicago's Drake Hotel. I suggested that she send the children with the nanny while we took a leisurely drive to Chicago together. We could do it easily in two or three days. She was delighted.

That first afternoon, we reached San Francisco and checked into a hotel. The following afternoon, we went to see a much-acclaimed film that we had both missed. When we came out of the theater the streets were dark. The Japanese had bombed Pearl Harbor.

Unfortunately, we were not "made for each other." To put it another way, she was not a soul mate. The trip might have been a high point considering that finally, I was not alone. It turned out to be a low point, the further irony being that Marsha was a companion who failed to ease the ache. I was still alone.

We crossed the Rockies and then on to the plains of Nevada. The roads were long and straight. One could comfortably drive ninety miles an hour. One night, in the distance, we could see a red light on the road. Marsha was temporarily at the wheel. She was so anxious to see what was happening up ahead that she forgot to slow down. By the time she decided to use the brake it was too late, and she smashed into the back of a car that had been backing up. The front of my beautiful New Yorker convertible was damaged, as was the car we hit, although the damage was not catastrophic.

When we arrived in Chicago, Buddy gave us a royal welcome. I couldn't help wondering why he was so very friendly. After my lonesome stay in Beverly Hills, it was a pleasant experience to be hosted so graciously by, at the moment, Chicago's number-one show business celebrity.

Before leaving Chicago, I phoned ahead to Charles Hazelet in Pittsburgh. Charles was one of the men, several years my senior, whom I had met at Bill Brown's Physical Training Farm. I invited him to join me for dinner at the hotel when I reached Pittsburgh. After dinner he said, "I want to show you something." We got into his car and he drove me to Pittsburgh's Lincoln dealer. There, in the window, beautifully lit, was the new 1942 Lincoln Continental convertible. It was, at the time, one of the world's most beautiful automobiles. The Lincoln symbol on the hood was gold plated, as were the door handles and the hubcaps. It was a singular thing of beauty – I loved it and I wanted it. Charles had wanted to buy it but the deal they gave him was unacceptable, so he turned it down. Now he just wanted me to see it. The car was indeed beautiful; whoever designed it put Picasso's *Two-Faced Ladies* to shame.

The next morning I made a deal right on the spot, exchanging my lightly damaged Chrysler for this new dream car. Of the many cars that I have owned there was only one other that gave me the same high every time I looked at it, and that was my 1955 seven-passenger Rolls Royce limousine with its running boards and huge headlights. Subsequently Charles learned that I had bought the car and phoned me in New York. He was livid. I was astonished. He had made it clear that the price of the car was more than he would pay, about $4,500.

My beautiful Lincoln Continental notwithstanding, I was still utterly miserable. When I got back to New York, Betty was still there and we resumed our affair. However, the romance was gone and Betty said that she could not continue to stay with me under the circumstances. It was a friendly but sad ending. I have always respected Betty for her courageous behavior. It took a strong woman to walk away from what might appear to have been a cushy situation. Stupid boy. Betty had probably found a new boyfriend during my six-month leave of absence.

The lease on my penthouse apartment was up and I moved to One Fifth Avenue, an elegant residential hotel. I had a handsome three-room apartment on the nineteenth floor: a huge living room with five windows and three exposures, a cozy bedroom, a bath, and a kitchen. I looked straight down on historic Washington Square Park with its handsomely designed archway that marks the beginning of Fifth Avenue.

Nevertheless, I was so miserable I needed a psychoanalyst. Doctor Leonard Blumgart had been highly recommended by Mack Lipkin, my doctor. Blumgart was a handsome, reserved, well-spoken man who had no trouble making me feel comfortable. He was also president of the New York Psychoanalytic Association. He explained that a Freudian analysis required five visits a week. My businessman's brain told me that two visits a week would pay for double the number of weeks I would be in therapy, and there was nothing he could say that would persuade me to change my mind. I had sessions twice a week but nothing much happened. Nevertheless, Blumgart said I was one of his two most successful patients. Walter Lippmann, at that time the country's best-known serious columnist, followed me as Blumgart's next patient. I met him accidentally: I was going out and he was coming in.

These were of course the years of World War II and all over the world people's lives were being destroyed. Though my own problems seemed trivial in comparison, it was not until much later that I could see my life in better perspective.

9

In 1942, I Open the Mortimer Levitt Gallery

Back in 1927, Lee Cohen, my sailing partner, introduced me to Victor Thall III. Victor had just returned from Paris, one of the many American expatriate artists who moved there because the dollar was so strong. Victor, a painter, was the handsome, charming fellow who also introduced me to Ernest Hemingway's novel, *The Sun Also Rises*, which at that time was a glimpse into another world.

Fifteen years later, in 1942, Victor introduced me to Johannes Schiefer, another painter. Schiefer, in turn, introduced me to his small group of Greenwich Village friends, all artists, mostly painters: Adolpho Saporetti, Oronzo Gasparo, and the O'Connor brothers, Patrick and Roderic. Unfortunately, they were selling very few paintings and there were stacks of unsold canvases in each studio. All five had works in museum collections and all five did representational painting. In some ways, they were behind the cutting edge because non-objective paintings had come to the fore.

The San Remo Café in Greenwich Village was our gathering place. It really was a bar, with two tables in front and six tables in the back. That's where we frequently met for dinner. The men were constantly bemoaning their fate. I started thinking about their problem, and, *surprise, surprise,* I came up with an idea. I remembered how depressed I had been in the Hotel Russell suite the night Annie and I agreed to separate. I was in a gloomy mood, of course, but the suite itself was gloomy and I had wondered why. At that moment, I remembered that I'd decided it was because of the paintings – there weren't any. The few unlit prints they had on the walls were no substitute for the paintings that came with Annie. Those were mostly paintings by Aline, my mother-in-law, plus a full-color reproduction, handsomely framed and well lit, of Van Gogh's portrait of "Man in a Straw Hat" that hung over our fireplace.

I had concluded that an apartment without paintings on its walls, without books and without any evidence of music, lacked any feeling of culture –it was an apartment without character. Paintings, therefore, to my mind at least, were as important to a living room as chairs, sofas, and tables. Then came the question of how to get those unsold paintings onto the walls that so badly needed them.

The concept: I would open a gallery and give each artist a one-man show. But my gallery would be different. I explained to the boys that realistically supply and demand determine price levels. If they would drop their sky-high prices to a realistic level - let's say $250 for a twenty by twenty-four oil painting - that would be an advantageous price.

But how could I reach the people who had those empty walls? After considerable head scratching, I concluded that they could be reached through decorators. I could well afford a persistent yet elegant direct mail campaign to decorators, explaining first the obvious, that an apartment needed paintings to give it character. Equally important, I would pay decorators the same commission they now received on furniture. Nevertheless, our prices would still be below the market, including their commission. The easiest target would be those who were redoing an apartment or furnishing a new apartment. The decorators would pay attention because obviously, our message was different from that of the other Fifty-Seventh Street galleries.

I opened up what turned out to be one of New York's most beautiful galleries at 16 West Fifty-Seventh Street, calling it the Mortimer Levitt Gallery. I had the walls painted *café au lait*, a warm and neutral background for framed paintings. Almost every painting would be expensively framed. That would be handled quite simply, as I ordered a large group of expensive frames in standard size (12x14, 16x20, 20x24, 24x30, and 30x40). If my artists would use canvases in standard sizes (they usually do), potential buyers could see each painting to its best advantage because every one is beautifully framed. I thought of it as enlightened merchandising.

In 1942, I Open the Mortimer Levitt Gallery

The Mortimer Levitt Gallery, 16 West 57th Street, 1942.
Photos missing: three rooms, office, and storage.

The decorator would bring the client and tell us the approximate sizes they wanted to see. Most important, our paintings were priced under the market and all of our painters were represented in museums. It was, in effect, a bonanza for the client, a bonanza for the decorator, and a bonanza for the artists. There was one additional attraction: there would be no bargaining, unlike other galleries where the asking price was usually only a starting point. Our prices would be listed and authentic. If demand went up, our prices would go up. Prices varied, depending upon the artist and the size and did not include the frames, which sometimes were almost as expensive as the painting. We also carried a small collection of watercolors but the main business of the gallery was oil paintings.

It seemed like a wonderful idea, so why wasn't business better? Because decorators and clients wanted names. An ugly Picasso, a mediocre Matisse, or an unlikely Cezanne would sell for fifty to a hundred times the price of an attractive oil painting by a still relatively unknown artist. Yet the paintings that grace the rooms in our two homes are, by my choice, undiscovered artists. Fortunately, they are paintings I still enjoy and their anonymity adds individuality to our collection.

I became deeply disenchanted with the art world because collectors are like sheep. Van Gogh sold only one painting in his lifetime. Those unsold paintings were no more beautiful in 1945 than they were in 1885, yet in the eighties and nineties Van Gogh was selling for millions of dollars – one painting sold for forty million.

To simplify, here's a more up-to-date view: In 1942, famous-to-be painters of our time, for instance, de Koonig, Rothko, and Jackson Pollock, were also sitting with studios full of unsold canvases. Once the Museum of Modern Art bought or accepted a painting as a gift from a collector, the acceptance acted as certification of quality, and prices skyrocketed. Today, those paintings too, are selling in the millions. Almost overnight, the artist then is established and his paintings sell at double, triple, and even quadruple. When I became involved with the world of painting, I was seeing only the aesthetics. Subsequently, I discovered that museum curators and the collectors were mostly seeing the signature at the bottom.

Peggy Guggenheim opened her kooky gallery next to mine and called it *Art of this Century* (a twist on the expression "out of this world"). Peggy's gallery was designed by Kiesler and there was no other gallery quite like it. I can explain it best by saying that it had the "quirkiness" of Disneyland. "Eccentric Peggy" featured Jackson Pollack, a non-selling alcoholic drip painter. Peggy lived to have the gratification of seeing Jackson Pollack's work sold for some $3 to $5 million dollars. As I saw it, the art world was not really dealing with aesthetics, but rather the lure of collecting. For the *nouveau riche* collecting paintings of well-known artists was a social asset, a step up the ladder. Museum curators followed along. It seemed that the collectors set the tone.

My gallery had been open three years when we received a phone call from *Fortune* magazine. They were doing a piece on the Fifty-Seventh Street galleries, at that time the center of our art world. The gallery director and I were invited to the Plaza for a drink and an interview. The two writers doing the interview were so fascinated by our concept, they invited us to stay on for dinner because there was so much to talk about.

In 1942, I Open the Mortimer Levitt Gallery

Their article appeared in the magazine two months later, and this was the last sentence of the final paragraph: "… and then there was also the Mortimer Levitt Gallery, but certainly there were tax benefits." Where in the world could that have come from? My gallery was indeed different from any other gallery on Fifty-Seventh Street; we were together for three hours because our story was well worth telling; and certainly there were **no** tax benefits. That was obviously an editor's melodramatic intrusive twist, possibly an editor I had at some time inadvertently offended.

I chose as director a woman who ran a frame shop and had previously been the artistic director of a Midwest art center. She was quite familiar with the art world and her appointment as the Gallery's director would give it a much-needed certificate.

I think now that it would have been much better to have turned the gallery over to Mimi, my second wife. We would have been brilliantly successful. As a result of her long experience at the Museum of Modern Art, Mimi knew what to buy, who to buy, where to buy it, and how much to pay. And unlike me, she was enamored of non-objective painting. I would have been the un-proud owner of a successful gallery but I possibly would have lost my lovely wife to one of those untidy, egocentric painters. Although *Fortune* gave the gallery an ignominious quote, the gallery had put me into *Who's Who In America*. The gallery, as conceived, was really much needed. Unfortunately, it was only partially successful and I closed it after twelve years in 1955.

10

The High Life

As a bachelor, retired from the day-to-day management of my beloved business, I became a wanderer. All in all, I had four years of traveling, and that's a lot of traveling. In November of 1945, right after the end of the World War II, I started off on a six-month trip to Egypt and the Middle East. I came back to the United States for six months and left again in the fall of 1946 for another six-month trip, this time to Europe, including London, Paris, and the south of France. I met Mimi when I returned home, and after some fourteen months, I realized that finally I had fallen in love. I asked her to marry me.

In the fall of 1948, we were off on a one-year honeymoon, mostly all over Europe, with a month in Egypt. In the years after our honeymoon, we also took many shorter trips that lasted four, five, or even six weeks. However, this is not a travelogue, and the details of my various trips will be reserved, possibly, for a magazine piece. But for now, I'll outline several memorable incidents that are worthy of repetition.

* * * * * *

In the summer of 1945, I spent three weeks in Nantucket at the White Elephant Inn. There I had the good fortune to meet Richard Dreyfus (Swiss Bank Dreyfus) and his new wife Denise. Denise Moserri (Swiss-born, but raised in Cairo) had been living here during the war earning graduate degrees at Columbia University. They had a lovely little girl named Catherine, who was eighteen months old.

The High Life

One night we were having dinner together shortly after Japan surrendered. Denise said, "Mortimer, Richard and I will be sailing back to Cairo in November. You are doing nothing, why don't you come with us?" Well, why not? I was single, had an art gallery, was self-made, self-educated, and let's say, an American novelty for these European-born semi-aristocrats. It was the beginning of a lifetime friendship. Denise's grandfather had founded the Bank Mosseri in Cairo and her father inherited the bank. He bought the King David Hotel in Palestine and several other hotels and large plantations growing top-grade Egyptian cotton. Denise's father had died in 1943, leaving Denise and her beautiful Greek stepmother, Helene, his magnificent mansion on the Nile.

I expected to be in the Middle East for six months so it made sense to bring my beautiful Lincoln convertible (automobiles were accepted as luggage). I had a lovely stateroom shared with Hans Rueshe, a writer. Our arrival in   Alexandria was akin to watching a three-ring circus. The dock was a bedlam of thin men, short by United States standards, all clamoring out loud with imploring gestures, begging for the privilege of carrying our personal luggage off the boat. The luggage taken on a sixteen-day sea voyage is apt to be heavy. I'll never get over the sight of those little men, many of them quite old, who, despite their frailty, could put a rope around a steamer trunk and carry it down the gang plank on their backs.

Although the English were still in charge Egypt's second language was French. Back then, as an American projecting the image of an Englishman, I could walk through native quarters without fear, unmolested, as opposed to walking through Harlem, Watts, or other ghetto areas in the United States.

Shortly after our arrival, Denise gave a party in honor of King Farouk in the Moserri mansion. It was rumored that Denise's stepmother, Heline, had an affair with the King who had earned the reputation of a womanizer. At one point, the King, (a "man of the people") seated himself on the floor with his back to the wall. He was not prepossessing: too pale, and already losing much of his sandy-colored hair. At this time, he had not yet put on those additional one hundred and forty pounds. A male confidant was seated to his left, while three other men sat on the floor facing him in a semicircle. There was room for one more so I (timidly? boldly?) joined the group. The conversation was in French and much too fast for me. My sitting there for some ten minutes without saying a word compelled the King to ask in English, "Who is this sad sack?" For a moment, I was back in Brooklyn. I said, "My name is Mortimer Levitt and Denise is my friend. Unhappily, I speak little French." What I lacked back then was the ability to give an insolent response in French. I had not yet learned to "Keep Smiling."

* * * * * *

Denise had arranged for me to become a non-resident member of the Gazeera Sporting Club (no Arabs admitted) so I could enjoy my tennis and enlarge my meager social horizon. The one meeting of consequence turned out to be with Mademoiselle Helene Duc (pronounced Duke), a French actress who was in Cairo with the Comédie Francaise, France's National Theater. We became a couple.

I went to the Gazeera Club frequently to play tennis. One day, while waiting for my tennis teacher, I talked with a woman, a *Grande Dame* I had met at Denise's party. In the course of conversation, I said "I'll be forty next month," at which she exclaimed, "No! No! You don't look like forty and you don't say you're forty until you look it beyond any doubt." Cairo society, considered elegant, was to my eye, provincial. My teacher was ready and we went to the court.

He was an excellent teacher who worked much harder than our tennis teachers in Connecticut. In any case, he stopped in the middle of the lesson, excused himself, walked to the corner of the court, unrolled a prayer rug, and there in the bright Cairo sunshine, kneeled down and prayed to Allah. When he finished, he rolled up his prayer rug and we continued the lesson. I was told he did that six times a day and I couldn't help observing that Allah, evidently, made more demands than Jesus. However, I never made it a point of conversation, possibly because I was getting results.

* * * * * *

I thought it best to continue my French lessons at Berlitz in Cairo but most of the French I learned came from my relationship with Helene, as her English was no better than my French. She expanded her English vocabulary and I expanded my French. Helene had decided not to return to Paris with the troupe, and joined me on a trip up the Nile, to Aswan and Luxor, followed by a trip through the Middle East.

Mademoiselle Helene Duc in Cairo avec M. Mortimer in Egypt.

Driving across the desert was eerie; there was no traffic, we were out there all alone. At one point we got out of the car, walked over a small sand dune, took off our clothes. I thought it was a smashing idea to take photographs in the desert that would add an exotic touch to our albums. Obviously, I was not nearly as sophisticated as I thought because the photographs were all out of focus.

Helene had her *Guide Bleu* so we touched all the *Jesus places* –Helene was Catholic. We had been together for some six weeks, much of which was spent touring the Middle East. Now we were returning to Cairo. We were stopped at the border, a dilapidated shack barely big enough to seat two unprepossessing guards. The shack was set in the middle of nowhere in the desert. Unexpectedly they asked for our passports. Horrors!

It turned out that Helene's passport was just outdated, so we couldn't pass. They both rejected a bribe. However, they permitted us to phone our several "big shot" friends in Cairo. Helene called hers and I called mine, but with no luck. We were stopped dead in our tracks and Palestine was far behind us. Panic!

The senior guard saved the moment; his wife was on vacation and he would be happy to have us as his guests overnight. We were both reluctant yet happy to be offered the apartment of which he was, obviously, so proud. It was the ultimate in cheap kitsch. He gave us clean sheets for the double bed in which he and his wife slept. At some point in the night when we were having sex we discovered why the guard had been so generous. He was standing in the corner, a peeping tom and quiet as a mouse.

When we realized he was standing in the doorway, sex flew out the window and he lost any chance he had in mind for joining the party. Fortunately, he was not a bully so we, all three, returned to what we should be doing in the first place, sleeping. The next morning a call came through from a high government friend of Helene and we were permitted to pass through the border. The whole thing was so out of context, it was surreal – it didn't happen, but it did. Picture if you can that ancient, insignificant shack in the desert as a front line.

* * * * * *

I went back to New York for my customary six months, and in October of 1946, I booked passage on the USS Constitution for a six-month European trip. I had once again expected a cabin for two. To my horror, the cabin turned out to be a huge room that had accommodated some thirty soldiers in double bunk beds. I was so shocked in realizing that there was no backing out, it almost brought tears to my eyes. I recovered quickly and immediately grabbed an outside upper bunk.

As it turned out, there was compensation: a really beautiful twenty-three-year-old, healthy, blue-eyed, California blonde (not a sex pot), who was going to Switzerland to teach English to students who spoke *Shfitser Duetch*. This was an unexpected affair, you might say, from heaven. I knew that Helene was being driven from Paris to welcome me off the boat. Nevertheless I invited Carolyn to join me for a six-week trip through the South of France. Unfortunately, she had a contract she couldn't break, so we kissed each other good-bye and I kissed Helene hello. The romance with Helene had come to an end. It was now, in my mind, downgraded to friendship.

Subsequently, I learned that Carolyn had married a Swiss man, they were living in Zurich. When Mimi and I were on our honeymoon, we invited them out for dinner (his name was Helmuth), along with another couple. We were a party of six and it was fascinating that one citizen would be the designated driver and would strictly observe the no-alcohol rule. In this regard, they were miles ahead of the United States.

In 1987, forty-one years later, I answered the telephone in our New York home and the cracked voice of an old lady said, "Is this Mr. Levitt, Mortimer Levitt?" I said, "Yes." And she said, "Oh Mortimer, I have been trying to reach you for years, and I couldn't remember the name of your business. This is Carolyn, how are you?" The ending of a cheap paper novel flashed through my brain. A California girl makes the mistake of marrying a Swiss gentleman. Because he lacks humor, she is penalized with an unrewarding marriage. Oh, if she had only taken that trip through the South of France with that amusing, interesting New Yorker, sexy to boot, and, and … a sad story akin to tragedy.

* * * * * *

When Mimi and I started our honeymoon, we stayed at the Ritz in Paris for the first six weeks. We had friends -Mademoiselle Helene Duc on the Left Bank and Richard and Denise on the Right Bank- and we spent several weekends in Denise's country home in Margency, a suburb of Paris. We enjoyed our time in Paris; the Ritz really is an exquisite hotel, a hotel for the elite as it has only two hundred and fifty rooms. It is always difficult to book a room at the Ritz and in those days, one needed an introduction. Denise made it possible.

We will skip our adventures in Lisbon, Madrid, and our trip along the Mediterranean to reach the Palace Hotel in Saint Moritz, where we had one month of skiing and a second month of skiing in Arosa. After Arosa, we were guests in Denise's palatial mansion on the Nile. Even though it was late in the season, I took Mimi for a trip up the Nile to Aswan and Luxor; Mimi also wanted to see

Alexandria. I had read two enchanting novels that took place in Alexandria, so off we went for an overnight stay.

The next morning we hired a *fiacre* (a horse and carriage) to take us through the native quarter. We hadn't known that King Farouk's status was precarious, as was that of the English. A month before our arrival an English tourist couple had been stoned to death by a Muslim mob in a suburb of Cairo. The top of our carriage was down and we were going blithely along through the native quarter, a bazaar really, of open-air shops when I said, "Oh, look Mimi." Up ahead a white hearse, drawn by two white horses, had turned into our road.

As I had a camera in my hand, I stood up and took two shots. Suddenly, a native jumped at the carriage from my side, yelling at me in Arabic, even spitting in my face. He then tried to pull me out of the carriage. The driver had stopped the horse and out of the corner of my eye, I saw two policemen walk through the crowd without giving us a second look. Like ants in an anthill, we had been surrounded by a mob.

The situation was frightening, with me futilely pleading innocence, when from out of nowhere a man dressed in suit, shirt, and tie grabbed the overheated Arab, berated him and threw him away from the carriage. He quickly explained to us in French that when you photograph a dead baby you take the soul away from the body. We have no idea who our savior was only that he told the driver to continue and the crowd to disperse. I thought we would continue, but Mimi said, "Get us out of here!" No hero, I was lucky. And that was as close to death as I have ever been. A tragedy was averted because an anonymous person was there, at that moment, and had the courage to take such dangerous action.

* * * * * *

In 1965 we joined Marty Segal and his wife, Edith, for a six-week trip to Israel for the gala opening of the Shrine of the Book in Jerusalem. En route to Israel, we first flew to Sicily, a hair-raising experience. The plane had to fly through a precipitous pass to get to the airport. Rocks on either side seemed to be not more than ten feet from either wing and the air was turbulent.

The High Life

We had dinner with friends in Palermo and then continued on to Taormina, a venerable beachside resort that saw its popularity triple after Tennessee Williams, Truman Capote, and their friends chose it for summer vacations. It is an ancient town, intimate and charming. I was attracted to the bust of a Pope sculpted in wood and covered in tired-looking gold leaf. I saw it in the window of an antique store; it was very, very old. I found it irresistible. Incidentally, I couldn't get ten cents off the price, and adding insult to injury, I had to pay for the shipping. The almost life-size bust of that Pop, now sits on a pedestal in our dining room, partially blocking my view of our garden. He is there, morning, noon, and night, watching me eat while muttering to himself, "Lucky Mortimer."

* * * * * *

While driving back to Palermo, we stopped off to visit Mount Vesuvius. To begin with, Marty thought it was time for him to do his share of the driving, even though, in their family, Edith did all the driving. It was a bad idea, since we were at that point driving up to the base of Mount Vesuvius and the road was sharply curved. It was incredible that Marty, bright and efficient as he is, did not recognize his own incompetence at the wheel. When Mimi protested almost hysterically, Marty turned the wheel over to Edith.

It was a cold, dreary, windy day, so windy that the funicular was not working and we had to make the ascent in an open-air Jeep. The slope was covered with the remains of a snowfall. There were endless soot-covered ripples, each about ten inches high, similar to a series of small waves on water caused by wind. The totally barren, soot-covered landscape was akin to being on the moon. The eerie ambiance (not a tree, not a shrub), mixed with the wind, the gloom of heavy clouds, and topped by a dormant volcano that was still smoking, created a picture strong enough for instant recall in my slippery memory.

* * * * * *

We arrived at the King David Hotel with two days to spare. Our long-time friend, Armand Bartos, an architect, was the co-designer of the shrine that would house the Dead Sea Scrolls. He was there to welcome us. There were two other friends: Billy Rose, Broadway's shortest and much-acclaimed producer of musical extravaganzas; and Gordon Bunshaft, who designed Lever House, an internationally acclaimed building on Park Avenue. I don't like the Lever House, but that's another story. Gordon is known to his friends as Bun.

Billy had given Israel a sculpture garden adjacent to their new museum of art. It would exhibit many of Billy's sculptures and he had engaged Isamu Noguchi, a famous Japanese sculptor, to design it. However, Billy had a problem and asked Bunshaft and me for an opinion. Noguchi had molded Billy's flat acre of land into a thing of beauty. I was, shall I say, stage struck. It was so unexpectedly beautiful, and that was before any sculpture was even installed.

Billy wanted to use white marble chips for the pathways but Noguchi wanted black pavement. Billy asked us, "What do you think?" I jumped in, "It must be white marble chips. Black would absorb the sun's rays, making the sculpture garden too hot for comfort." Bun agreed. Billy called Noguchi over and said, "Tell the contractor to use the marble chips." Noguchi said, "You tell him, it's your sculpture garden," and walked away. Noguchi wasn't smiling, another artist's contempt for the patron assumed to be a Philistine. Poor Billy.

* * * * * *

One night, Mimi said, "Let's do Scandinavia," and I said, "Why not?" Our first stop was Stockholm, where we felt completely at home and on our first night, we had dinner at the home of friends. Our hotel was facing the Grand Plaza. On the opposite side the Opera House was celebrating the opening of a new and most elegant opera restaurant to which we took our friends.

In Denmark, we had looked forward to visiting Copenhagen's famous Tivoli Garden, a cross between Luna Park in Coney Island and the Luxembourg Gardens in Paris. It was April but the park doesn't open until the first week of June, so not to be outdone, we decided to visit Finland and try Helsinki's equally famous sauna. That was a real adventure.

The sauna took place on the top floor of our hotel, one section for men and another for women, with saunas by appointment only. I was shocked to be greeted by a woman who weighed between two hundred and fifty and three hundred pounds. She was all in white and the lower half consisted of a Turkish towel tightly held together with an oversized, safety pin. As requested, I took off my robe and pajamas, put them in a locker, was given a Turkish towel and a fresh cake of soap, and told to get into the shower. I was then shown into the hot room. The heat, generated by hot rocks, is very, very dry. I stretched out on a long wooden bench with a pillow for the head. From time to time, Butch would come in and beat me with Birch leaves. I said, "Hey what's that for?" She said, "We have to keep the blood running."

She came in again and said, "It's time for your massage." I really don't like massages but I remember vividly that massage as it was extended in between each one of my toes, on both feet. The massage was indeed inclusive. Then came another shower to get rid of the oil, and another session in the hot room. I had been told that it was then time to run out and roll naked in the snow. But instead, I was placed, not too carefully, in a huge ice-cold tank, an oversized bathtub. I was taken out, dried thoroughly, encased in a white cotton robe, and led to a cot in a small atrium with fresh sheets, fresh pillowcases, and a white wool blanket. I have never been so relaxed. It was so unexpected and so very special, that you might think I would have done it again and again, somewhere in the United States, but I am a relatively lazy man and the sauna required work, time, and patience. I was happy to have had such a singular experience, but never again.

* * * * * *

On that trip we also traveled to Russia, memorable mainly because I enjoyed talking with our various guides. We spent three weeks there, including Odessa, in the south, from which Russian Jews migrated. In 1962, one did not travel unattended so we were getting the party line first hand. But I had been well grounded in the principles of Communism, thanks to the classes held in Annie's apartment in 1936 and 1937. I was able to tweak the guides in regard to the many failed things that had been promised.

Our first night in Moscow we had been booked into a suite, which, crazy as it may sound, had a grand piano in the living room. In contrast, the toilet seat was broken, the food was awful, and the service was third rate. Mimi and I were alone, because we did not travel with a group.

A close friend had given us the name and phone number of a writer, daughter of a well-known Russian ambassador no longer alive. When Mimi phoned, naming our mutual friend, the response was very hush-hush. "Mimi, tell me what you'll be wearing." Mimi said, "I'll be wearing a brown fur jacket, boots, and a white fur hat." Irina said, "I will look for you when you come out of the elevator and we will greet each other like old friends. I will take you to our home for a drink." When we got to their apartment house, we walked up two flights of stairs. Her apartment opened to a small entryway, a plain unpainted wooden floor, with a tiny bedroom to the right and a small kitchen straight ahead. Her husband, a painter, took our coats. There was no living room, but a sumptuous spread had been set on the kitchen table around which we were comfortably seated.

We look unhappy, but we loved Moscow, 1962.

The High Life

They had two daughters, ages ten and twelve. I was surprised that husband and wife were raging against the administration while the children were still in the room. After the girls retired to their own room, I said, "How could you criticize the government so openly in front of your children?" The answer was, "Many of our friends have been carted off for saying things much less controversial than the things we have said tonight. We take a fatalistic view and speak our minds."

Irina and her husband were happy to meet another American couple that might resolve a problem. She asked us to smuggle two of her articles out of the country and give them to her publisher whose offices were in London. We did, and there was no problem.

* * * * * *

In the seventies, Mimi and I made two trips to South America. In 1973, Glenn Bernbaum suggested that I go to Columbia and maybe straighten out the problems we were having with a contractor who was making our custom-made slacks. The trip was uneventful except for the visit to Bogotá's modern museum, with the museum's president. The city of Bogotá is located on a high plain, some four thousand feet high, surrounded by mountains on four sides. Our hotel was located on a corner of the plain. On those many days that were not windy, automobile fumes drifted into the lobby of our hotel. It was, in a word, offensive. The fumes were trapped, surrounded as they were, by mountains.

I did what I had to do with the contractor and we went on to Peru. In Peru, our objective was Machu Picchu. We took a short flight from Lima up to Cuzco (eleven thousand feet), where we took a single-track train to the base of Machu Picchu, a two-hour ride. A group of Volkswagen busses inched up the vertical face of that shear wall, making hairpin turns even sharper than those in the Grand Canyon. Maybe it seemed sharper because the donkeys had four feet with which to make a turn. The Volkswagen busses were longer, making the turns more difficult and even more precarious.

Tourists usually make the Machu Picchu roundtrip in one day but we, along with a few others, elected to spend the night at the Machu Picchu hotel. On a scale of one to ten, the hotel had a rating of minus two. The next day, our train was due at 11:40 in the morning but a telegram came through saying there would be no train because it had been stopped by a landslide. Happenstance gave us a second day and a second night with a mixed bag of some twenty tourists. Mimi organized the tourists into a group, a dinner party, after which everyone was obligated to entertain; Mimi was the emcee. Perhaps six in the group had hiked from Cuzco.

Those two nights at Machu Picchu will never be forgotten; Machu Picchu by itself is, a wonderment! We were at the top of a canyon and you could hit the opposite side with a golf ball and a nine iron. How could those Indians have built a village in such a precarious spot? How could they have pushed around the rocks necessary to build their small houses, and how could they find enough soil to grow the wheat needed for bread? Machu Picchuis another one of life's endless mysteries.

As I see it, Machu Picchuis on a par with Carlsbad Caverns, the Grand Canyon, Cairo's Pyramids, and China's buried army sculptured in clay, with some of the soldiers even sculpted on horseback. "The creative mind of man takes life to the extreme by endlessly doing the impossible."

* * * * * *

Mimi suggested that we go to Rio and made the necessary arrangements. Rio's waterfront, which looked so incredibly beautiful in photographs, turned out to be a deep disappointment. That magnificent waterfront had been defaced by a ten-lane highway adjacent to the beach, with nothing separating the two. The beaches had no facilities of any kind – no showers, toilets, chairs, umbrellas, nothing – and at one end of the beach, raw sewage could be seen running across the sand into the ocean. The climate was miserable: hot, humid, sticky, and damp. The Grand Palace Hotel had lost its splendor and was drenched with an overpowering smell of mildew. The famous Brazilian beauties, if indeed they were there, totally escaped my eye.

We do have one happy memento of that trip. Rio is well known for its goldsmiths and for its semiprecious stones. We had two pieces of jewelry custom-made: a gold necklace with *perido* rubies and a pair of matching earrings. The necklace must be seen to be fully appreciated. Let's just say Mimi seldom wears it without receiving compliments on its unique design and understated elegance. It looks like a beautiful antique.

11

I Meet Mimi and

My Real Life Begins

My real life started when I met Mimi. It was October of 1947, and believe me, it was long overdue. I had just returned from my solo six months in Europe and had been invited to a cocktail party by Lolo Heinemann, a friend of the hostess. The front door opened onto a small foyer that faced a rather large dropped living room, and Lolo introduced me to the hostess. I looked around the room carefully before stepping down. Mimi, who at first glance reminded me of Ingrid Bergman, was at the furthermost corner engaged in serious conversation with a man. Drawn by some intangible force, I walked directly to her and sat, uninvited, between the two.

I knew right away that Mimi was my kind of girl. Not only was she good-looking, she was bright. Her relatively short and curly hair was, and still is, quite distinctive. I soon learned that Mimi held an important position with MOMA, the Museum of Modern Art. She was secretary to the museum collections. As an art dealer, I was familiar with the museum and the current art scene. It was my misfortune that I enjoyed very little of what the museum exhibited. Alfred Barr was the museum's first director and Mimi worked for Barr (actually, they're on a first name basis). The museum was founded in large part with Rockefeller money, Abby Rockefeller's in particular. The glamour was Rockefeller's, the passion was Barr's, and so "MOMA" was born. Mimi worked very closely with Alfred and had absorbed much of that passion. So, of course, we were immediately at odds. Still, I enjoyed talking with her and knew I would see her again.

I Meet Mimi and My Real Life Begins

At the time, however, I was deeply involved in negotiations with Erwin Friedlander (Friedy) to buy DeFries, his handsome and successful store. Those negotiations were taking a lot of my time so I told Mimi she would hear from me in about four weeks.

Earlier that year, when I left Europe, I sold my Pontiac, just as I had sold my Lincoln when I left Egypt. The Lincoln cost about $4,300 and I sold it to a well-heeled Sheik for $10,000. I could not get immediate delivery of a new Lincoln, so I bought a secondhand car to tide me over: a Packard Phaeton. It was the longest car Packard had ever built. The Phaeton was generally used with the top down. It had a second set of windshields for those riding in the back seat, which was very spiffy. The car was simply beautiful. When Mimi saw that car she decided that I was either creative or romantic, and certainly more interesting than the Mortimer she had met at the cocktail party.

Our first date was not exactly a success. I was to pick Mimi up outside the museum at 6:00 in the evening, but there was no Mimi. She came walking along leisurely about twenty minutes late, dressed in a wrinkled gray flannel suit with white chalk stripes. It had been raining earlier in the day and it was humid. She had been out in the rain and she was, indeed, wrinkled. We got into the car and I said, almost immediately, "I don't usually go out with young girls." Mimi had just turned twenty-six and I had just turned forty.

"You knew we had a date tonight. I can't take you out dressed this way, as we will be dinner dancing at the Pierre. Would you mind changing your clothes?" Mimi had no objection. At the time she was living on Park Avenue in two rooms that had been built originally to house the servants of people living in the building. It was a basement apartment with two small windows.

The Pierre's Cotillion Room was one of New York's most beautiful and was perfect for dinner dancing. In addition, we were entertained by a mind-reading magician. I knew five minutes after we were on the dance floor that she meant more to me than I meant to her. As soon as we sat down, I asked an unanswerable question, quite stupid really, thus becoming even less interesting: "Why don't you like me as much as I like you?"

I don't remember anything about our second date but soon afterwards, Lisl Krauss, Mimi's Viennese high school friend, had been invited to spend a weekend in the country in the home of her new boyfriend. Mimi had also been invited and was asked to bring along a date. She extended the invitation to me. It was that weekend Mimi discovered "the man inside the man." I was a totally new experience for Mimi, her prior relationships having been with friends who were all more or less Bohemian.

Mimi had come to the United States in 1939 from Vienna with her mother, aunt, and grandmother (her father had already emigrated), just barely escaping Hitler's SS. In central Europe, Germany, and Austria, the Jewish population was divided. One part thought that the Jewish problem would be resolved with Israel, a Jewish state, and the other half thought the problem would be resolved with assimilation. This second half is the one Mimi's family belonged to. Her maternal grandfather was a Lutheran. Mimi's parents converted, and Mimi was baptized as a Lutheran. They settled in Los Angeles.

Mimi graduated Phi Beta Kappa from Pomona College. It is a cliché that opposites attract, but that's the way it was. Mimi is a giver; I cannot say that about myself, although I may be a giver in different ways. Should I misplace something, which I do frequently, Mimi takes the trouble to look for it. If I hurt, for whatever reason, Mimi wants to fix it because she is concerned.

It was not too long before Mimi and I were spending six nights together, but the seventh night belonged to Mimi. It would be that way until we were married.

It was now May of 1948 and Mimi had a three-week vacation due. She suggested we spend it in Los Angeles, as both her mother and sister lived there. I would stay at the Beverly Wilshire Hotel, and she would stay with her mother. So I said, "Mimi, dear, why don't we just get married?" Mimi burst into tears, thereby accepting my gallant proposal.

So, on the eighteenth of June, Mimi, who was a baptized Lutheran, and I, a more-or-less retired Jewish atheist, were married in the office of Dr. Jerome Nathanson, leader of the nonsectarian Ethical Culture Society. Our doctor, Mack

Lipkin, and his beautiful wife, Carol, witnessed the ceremony. When Mimi was required to say yes, she would accept me as her husband, she started to cry. Our doctor immediately supplied her with a handkerchief.

After the ceremony, we phoned our respective mothers and then took off for John Lurie's Burroughs View Club. John's place was beautifully located in Phoenicia, New York's Woodland Valley. This part of the Catskill Mountains was a New York State Park that had not yet been invaded by hotels. We went there for the weekend, bursting to tell John that we were just married, forgetting that the last time we were there we pretended that we were married. John's response to the good news was typical. "Don't you know that I don't permit unmarried couples to share the same bedroom? How could you do that to me?" We were humbled and I apologized.

May '49, Ten Heavenly Days in Capri.
I'm wearing gray velvet shorts and a black fisherman's turtleneck.

When we returned to New York, several problems had to be resolved. The first might be jokingly referred to as a prenuptial contract. We would take a year off to have a honeymoon. Mimi liked that part of the agreement. Our honeymoon was to last fifty-four weeks. Mimi would be obliged to give up her position at the museum; she didn't like that at all. My thinking went like this: I was forty, and it was time to have children and time to set up a home. Under those circumstances, it would be difficult for Mimi to pursue a serious career at the museum. Mimi compromised by giving Alfred three months notice.

At the track in Rome.

Mimi was also to stay out of my gallery, except for the various receptions that were given for the opening of each new show. If Mimi were to interfere with the gallery's director, it would mean squabbles. Mimi either had to be the director or stay out. Any advice she might have should be given to me, not to Ulla.

I said, "I'll get in touch with our travel agency." Mimi said, "You don't have to do that. I'll take care of it." And she did. So, we were off and running and that's when I found "the glory."

In the summer of 1950, we rented a house on the water (Long Island Sound) in Westport, Connecticut. In that same year, Mimi had become pregnant with Elizabeth. We were living in our apartment at One Fifth Avenue. I thought it would be a mistake to move into a larger apartment, and then, as our family grew, into a still larger one. Our marriage was solid, for real, and we should have our own home. Mimi agreed that we would buy a townhouse. We started our search in Greenwich Village. The Village is a relatively small area. We came up with nothing, so we extended our search to the Upper East Side.

I had one requirement: that the house be on the south side of the street so the sun could pour into the garden we would create. That cut our potential in half. Mimi believes we looked at some fifty houses but I was under the impression that we looked at some twenty before deciding finally. In January of 1951, we bought a townhouse on East Eighty-Second Street, a most desirable block, leading, as it did, to the main entrance of the Metropolitan Museum.

It was a five-story brownstone - six including a usable basement - so installing an elevator was essential. That meant moving walls on almost every floor. The grand staircase on the west wall would be eliminated and in that most desirable space we could put a kitchen and pantry. On the east wall we could create a lobby of generous size and convert the servant's staircase into a stairway suitable for guests. We were lucky to find an architect who had long experience in converting townhouses.

Elizabeth was born on the ninth of June in 1951, and for the second year we went again to Westport, this time renting the Bishop home for the summer. Mr. Bishop was Dean of the Law School at New York University. With us were Elizabeth, Miss Solomon, the children's nurse, and Mike, my Welsh terrier.

The Eighty-Second Street renovations took nine months and cost thirty percent more than we paid for the house. We got back from Westport in the middle of September but the house was by no means ready to receive us. We had a finished third floor, our bedroom, dressing rooms, two baths, Mimi's study, and a finished fourth floor, the children's floor. We had workmen in the house for the next two months finishing everything that still had to be done: the kitchen, dining room, library, terrace, garden, music room (salon), and the fifth floor, with two baths, two bedrooms for the servants, and my office, a sunny room overlooking the garden. The room that would be our son Peter's, the dining room, library, our bedroom, and my office were all on the sunny south side.

There was a three-floor extension in the back of the house originally used as a butler's pantry and extra bathroom. We tore the extension down so we could have a terrace and a full-size garden, twenty feet by forty feet. I designed the garden using only evergreens, so our garden is green year round. Our azaleas and rhododendrons begin blooming in early May, giving us a blaze of flowers in purple and red. That's when we start weekending in Westport. We move up for the summer around the tenth of June. So, we are filled with flowers both in our New York garden and in Westport.

Three years after we were comfortably installed, Mimi said, "Mortimer, you have an office downtown, why do you need an office here? Besides, a man should be out doing his own thing, not hanging around the house." I had no good answer. Whatever business I had to conduct was then conducted at the Custom Shop office, which in 1951 was located at 9 Desbrosses Street, one block below Canal and one block from the Hudson River. Our executive offices and workrooms were all on one nine-thousand-foot floor.

We were both happy with our completely renovated townhouse, happy with the layout the architect gave us, and happy with the décor, some of which was thanks to the know-how of Doris Dessauer, Walter Dessauer's wife. We made the rounds of the D&D Building with Doris. That brought us some of the furniture, the printed linens that covered the walls in the master bedroom, the library, and the bedrooms of Peter and Elizabeth.

The entire east wall of the library was filled with books in the walnut structure that we had custom built. The entire first shelf was filled with my record albums. We also had bookshelves in Peter's room, in Mimi's study, and in Elizabeth's room.

"Aren't you lucky! Very few people have anything original that's nice."
A friendly home needs paintings, etchings, drawings or posters on the walls.
COLLECTION OF THE AUTHOR.

All of the walls, including the entrance and the walls of the stairwell, were hung with paintings from my gallery. From time to time, new paintings were added, bought by Mimi, by me, or jointly. Then, having finished the exterior and the interior, we had a house. We had an ambiance but not yet a home. I had decided, in my own mind, that a house was not a home unless there were friends. Friends, excluding family, would be invited for dinner. Mimi agreed, reluctantly I must confess, to having two dinner parties a week, summer, winter, spring, and fall in New York and in our summer home.

In the early years, we were eight for dinner. When I realized how much time it took Mimi to invite guests, I suggested that I take over. I thought of a way to make a drastic cut in the time it took. A wife could not accept an invitation without first clearing it with her husband because so many husbands travel, so I decided to have my secretary clear it first with the husband's secretary, who in turn would clear it with the wife. The secretary would then call my secretary back with an acceptance. If a change was necessary, my secretary would work out new dates with me.

The focal point of our small dinner parties, aside from good food, was to practice, shall I say, "the gentle art of conversation." It works out better with six people. With eight people, we had four conversations going at once, and with six we were able to have one. Everybody gets a turn, even the quiet ones.

Ed Koch, New York's former mayor, was a master host. In his home, he usually had dinner parties for twelve. When we sat down at the table, the first course was already laid. The chef was then brought out and stood alongside the maid. The chef would tell us what we will be having for dinner. He would disappear and Koch took over, suggesting that each guest introduce himself and say a word or two about his activities. It worked like a charm. There was one conversation, without any side conversations, and we would talk about whatever it was each particular guest was doing. Koch would move us on to the next guest. Everyone had a turn, everyone was happy, and conversation was singular and interesting.

I would like to think that this was my idea but I remembered that Aline Hayes had dinner parties regularly, and so did Osmond and Helene Fraenkel. The

Fraenkels had a townhouse on West Eleventh Street, the Hayes on East Tenth. The Fraenkels' dinners were more modest, as there was no maid with white gloves and Osmond would do the carving. Oh, how I envied that ability. Osmond and Helene were both articulate and careful in matching their guests. The Fraenkels usually had six people, the Hayes, eight to ten.

We decided it would be pleasant to spend summers in the country. However, to do things right, I thought we should first visit all the places that we might consider. We checked out Greenwich, Stamford, and Westport in Connecticut. In Massachusetts, we looked at the Cape, Provincetown, Wellfleet, Truro, and the Islands of Nantucket and Martha's Vineyard. In Long Island we browsed Westhampton, Southampton, and Easthampton. And yes, there was one more: Deal Beach in New Jersey.

Westport was an easy winner. It was only sixty minutes by commuter train from the city. Located directly on the Long Island Sound, it had good beaches, good sailing, good golf, lots of tennis, and, most important, a unique mixture of interesting people. There was an above average sprinkling of men and women in show business, television, advertising, music, the arts, and more than a share of celebrities, including Leonard Bernstein, Jason Robards, Richard Rodgers, Joanne Woodward, and Paul Newman. Actually, I could name another ten or twenty. We never regretted our choice. For the first twelve years, we rented different homes because I did not want to own another house.

The family had grown. We now had Elizabeth, Peter, the nanny, Miss Solomon, and Mike, my Welsh terrier. Miss Solomon was with us for eight years. She was German, very experienced, the perfect nanny. She was sixty-six years old and still spry. Elizabeth spent two summers in France, Peter spent one summer in Spain. There were eight years with a German-speaking nanny and neither of them have spoken one word of German, not one word of Spanish, and Elizabeth's French makes me sound like a professor. Mimi is a linguist, but none of that was passed on to our children.

Our summer life settled into a happy routine and Mimi became the Longshore Club's Women's Golf Champion. The club, incidentally, is an amenity owned by the town and open to its citizens and their guests.

Mimi was a much better golfer than I could ever hope to be. Nevertheless, one day, out of nowhere, I shot an eighty-two. An eighty-two? Yes, an eighty-two. It was in Los Angeles and we were playing with Mimi's father and stepmother. I said, "Mimi, I'll never play golf again. I will not ruin my life chasing that eighty-two score." I gave my clubs away so I wouldn't be tempted. I switched from golf to tennis at an age when other men switch from tennis to golf.

Our beautiful pond. The rest of the pond is behind the photographer; Long Island Sound on the left, our house on the right.

Dana Lee, one of my most gifted sailing girls, took this snapshot on a fall afternoon, just before casting off.

I Meet Mimi and My Real Life Begins

I became an avid tennis player, playing six mornings a week in the summer, four mornings a week in spring and fall, and two mornings a week in winter when I move indoors. Early on, I discovered that playing with men was impossible. They were too good, too wild, or too fast. Aside from that, they were not available on weekdays. Playing with women was more enjoyable because they were less wild and less powerful. At one time, I had twenty-seven women on my tennis list in Westport, and eleven women on my New York list. I set up no steady games, which is why I needed the long list. When I was playing well, I went to the top of the list; when I was playing badly, I went to the bottom. When my game was normal, I called, in succession, the most personable.

I renewed my love for sailing after getting to know Bernie Green, the conductor-composer of the Wally Cox radio and television show *Mr. Peepers*. Bernie had a twenty-six-foot Herashoff S-Class sloop. He desperately needed a sailing companion and I was the one man free on weekday afternoons, the time Bernie preferred to go sailing. We sailed together for two summers, after which I bought my own sailboat, a Lightning. It was named *MIMO*.

Lightnings in 1952 were probably the largest racing sloop class in the country. Mimi complained, and rightly so, that sailing took her away from her golf. She said that it was not fair for me to take her away from her golfing (Mimi, in addition to being the two-time club champion, was also president of the Longshore Women's Golf Association). Mimi suggested that I get my own company for sailing. I had about fourteen girls on my sailing list and a man named Harvey Koizim. Then I had twenty-seven girls on my tennis list. Think of it as Mortimer's harem. I sailed five afternoons a week and reserved six mornings for tennis. As I had no set dates for sailing or tennis, that kept me out of any potential involvements.

It was about this time that I finally began to understand the depth of the girl I married. Mimi is a caring mother, generous, loyal, loving, and easily able to make friends and keep them. I could see that she engendered wide-ranging respect and I appreciated it doubly because, you might say, I found myself lacking. I don't want to exaggerate but the fact is that Mimi is more of a person than I will ever be, and it took me three or four years to realize that. Better late than never. (Love those clichés.)

In 1960, and again in 1962, Mimi and I rented a house in Westport close to the one we presently own. The house faced the water and was perched on a modest fifteen-foot hill. I drove past that house four times a day. It caught my fancy despite the fact that it was painted pink with black trim at the windows. I longed to see it from the inside. It was in 1962 that I discovered, quite accidentally, that the house had been on the market for the past year. As it turned out, the house was a converted barn.

Reenie Stein, then married to a successful lawyer *(Another phone call – Reenie just died of Alzheimer's)*, telephoned to say that she and her husband were guests of the Davidoff's and could we come over for a drink? The Davidoff's turned out to own the pink house facing the water, the very one that I had been so longing to see. It so happened on that particular weekend, Annie, my first wife, was staying with us. The three of us walked into that converted barn and directly facing us was an enormous picture window, eleven by fourteen feet. The view was spectacular, and I knew at once that we should buy it, so I concluded a deal with Dr. Davidoff almost immediately. The house was on three acres facing the water. The land tilted upward from sea level to about fifteen feet. In that situation, the fifteen feet improved the view immensely. After protracted negotiations, we bought the house completely furnished, and moved in on Labor Day.

We were immediately comfortable; any changes we might make could be done at a leisurely pace. The large screened-in porch was turned into a dining room with floor-to-ceiling thermopane windows on three sides. The Davidoffs had converted the barn into a *maison moderne*. The original beams looked uncomfortable in that setting. It would not be too difficult to change the image to one that was more in keeping with a traditional New England barn. As in most barns, there was a cathedral ceiling. Our living room was twenty-eight feet long and seventeen feet wide. There were not one, but two huge picture windows facing Long Island Sound. The window on the left was eleven by fourteen feet – enormous. The window on the right was six by nine feet. In between those two windows we placed our grand piano, directly opposite our handsome brick fireplace whose chimney stretched right up to the roof. The original beams were all weathered and visible. The hayloft held the master suite plus two bedrooms and two baths. We built a swimming pool alongside the dining room, and on the far side, four attractive cabanas, one for men and one for women, one for a shower, and one for a toilet. It was all just right, no mistakes – the servants had complete privacy and we had ours. We built a separate garage thirty-five feet from the house. It had an apartment above, two rooms and a bath that housed our staff, Fernando and Pepita, and their daughter, Rosemarie.

A slow stream moved across our front lawn. Dick Pistell, my friendly neighbor on the west, used the stream to dig out a huge pond. I joined him by continuing the pond onto our property, and I also paid to dig a pond for my neighbor on the east side. Their two homes were well back of mine, and not at all visible as we looked out onto Long Island Sound. In effect, their property was our property and their two ponds were also our ponds. All told, we had the illusion of owning thirteen acres.

Life continued to be interesting, there always something new. Our son, Peter was born fifteen months after Elizabeth. While the children were growing up, Mimi and I were able to continue the traveling that had ended with the honeymoon. What made travel possible was Miss Solomon and the fact that Mimi's mother moved in whenever we went on a trip. Mimi's mother was the kind of mother-in-law one hoped for, despite the mythical downside of mothers-in-law. Mutti was a doer, an avid tennis player, and a cultured woman who nurtured a love for opera in Mimi. She was progressive, politically aware, and, in short, quite unlike a mother-in-law.

Mimi and I were now well married and fortunately, in one way or another, traveling was not the end-all to our life. More importantly, we had dinner guests twice a week. After dinner, I would usually go to the piano and play for some ten minutes. Believe it or not, whenever I stopped, someone, sometimes two, would ask me to continue. As that happened consistently, I concluded that I was almost good enough to be a cocktail bar pianist.

12

Married Life:

After the Honeymoon

The upside, of course, was our two beautiful children: Elizabeth, born in June of 1951, and Peter, born in November of 1952. As it turned out, those beautiful children also created a downside. Mimi and I had been able to handle the usual domestic problems but we were miles apart when it came to raising children. Mimi loved our children and all transgressions were forgiven.

In contrast, I found myself cast in the role of the stern father. I was responsible and stable but evidently lacking in affection. I don't recall ever telling our children how much I loved them or having them say how much they loved me. So, it came to pass that we often found ourselves at odds: Mimi was very lenient, while I could not understand that a child is not a grown-up nor does he always need to be treated like a child. Unfortunately, the children put a minor blot on our marriage. I didn't know that, instead of getting better as they got older, they actually got worse until their early twenties. I didn't yet know about the teens. You might say I was green. In fact, I was dense.

I still can't get over the many twists and turns, good and bad, that take place in a life. One night, as we were going up to the third floor bedroom in our elevator, I began removing my smoking paraphernalia. I had started smoking cigarettes when I was sixteen, and at age eighteen I had taken up cigars and pipes. I later gave up the cigars but continued with the pipes. Now, I removed my pipe, my tobacco pouch, the pipe cleaner, my silver cigarette case, my Dunhill lighter, saying, "I really must quit smoking. I can't stand having all this junk in my pockets." Mimi said, "Why torture yourself? You know you have no will power." Twice before, I had tried to give up smoking. This was before smoking was determined to be a cause of cancer. Mimi's words did the trick. I gave up smoking to the point where I now resent anyone smoking in my presence.

Elizabeth is nine and Peter is eight.

Peter and Elizabeth – The teenage years.

I fell in love with the piano when I was four or five years old. It started when that man, whoever he was, played our piano at the one party we held at 436 Franklin Avenue. I was seven when I began taking piano lessons. However, the idea of reading two notes in the treble and three notes in the bass, or vice-versa, with both left hand and right hand playing different rhythms, was more than I could possibly cope with. Actually, I thought it was more than anyone could cope with; it seemed to me to be literally impossible. So with mother's permission, I switched to the violin. That was easy, because you had to read only one note at a time. I fondly remember the times we played the opening section of "The Poet and Peasant Overture," together, mother at the piano and I at the violin. Those were the only times I had real feelings of closeness with my mother.

One night in 1952, a dinner guest explained the concept of playing chords. One did not have to read four or five notes, but rather it was necessary only to read one thing, the chord name, before easily playing three or four notes, even five notes, without further reading. As it would not be necessary to read the individual notes, that sounded like something I could handle.

Subsequently, my eye caught a small advertisement in *The Sunday Times*: "Learn Piano by Ear – Steve Citron." Working with Steve was a pleasure. At the end of four years, I could sit down and play for one hour. Incidentally, I couldn't read music. All I had written were the chord sequences -the harmony. The melody was always in my head. I was taking ninety-minute lessons twice a week. I put a lot of expression into everything I played and that compensated to a large extent for a lack of technique. The songs I selected were melodic and relatively easy to play. They were mostly Richard Rodgers, George Gershwin, Cole Porter, et al. In addition, there were Three Chopin preludes, the third E minor, the sixth B minor, and the twenty-fourth C sharp minor, plus a small piece by Mozart, and "Varum," another by Schumann, that I loved particularly." And I loved to play the Prelude and Liebestod of Wagner's "Tristan Und Isolde."

After dessert, I would often get up from the dinner table and go to the piano. Our guests would then get the idea and Mimi would bring them into the music room. Guests seemed to enjoy my playing because someone would inevitably encourage me to continue after I stopped. I ended my piano lessons in 1956. I loved to play, but in 1990 I began to lose much of my technique. It is sad to say, but I had to stop. My left hand was trembling, my fingers no longer had their former authority, and to top it off, my impaired hearing distorted the sound. Playing could no longer bring me the musical high that I had once enjoyed.

Mimi and I were long-time skiers. We both started skiing about the same year, she was ten and I was twenty-four. Let me start at the beginning, as that was really the best part. It was my friend, Nat Levi, who invited me to join him for a weekend of skiing at John Lurie's Burroughs View Club. It was 1931 and for me, skiing was yet another new world.

Lurie's place was located in upstate Phoenicia's Woodland Valley– the lower Catskills. The house had originally belonged to a well-known naturalist named John Burroughs. A member of New York's Harmony Club later bought the house from the estate to use as a retreat for fishing and hunting.

The music room in our New York home, a far cry from Franklin Avenue

Every weekend in season, there would be half a dozen or so friends (no ladies) of the new owner at the house. John Lurie was also a member of the Harmony Club and he had befriended the owner. John's father brought Italy's Fiat automobile to the United States and he'd done well until 1929 when, along with so many others, he went bankrupt. John did his best to make it on Wall Street but that was not for him. At heart, John was a fisherman and a hunter. In fact, John inadvertently served as a guide and group leader. As a friend, he received no pay other than room and board. He loved living there full time and he inherited the house and the property when the owner unexpectedly died. With almost no income, Lurie decided to take paying guests. He named it Burroughs View Club, of which he was the owner and the host. One could be a paying guest, but only if introduced. If John didn't like you, you would no longer be welcome.

Recreational skiing was something new at that time. The first two winters there were no ski lifts, but John led a few of us up the trails that had been built by President Roosevelt's Civilian Conservation Corps (CCC). When we got to the top, we had a picnic lunch and then turned around to ski down. If we were going too fast, we just sat down. There were no steel edges, and bear trap bindings left much to be desired. But there is little that can compare with this incredibly beautiful and quiet world that opened us to skiing on those heavenly snow-covered CCC trails.

As a heavy smoker, climbing those trails was an enormous effort. But oh, how I loved it. Of all the places I have ever been on holiday, John's Burroughs View Club was, to this day, the most enchanting. And it was to this place that I brought Mimi when we were courting. For me, a city boy, it was an unexpected experience. A large barn separate from the main house had been renovated. John had a grand piano in the barn and he would play, not wonderfully, but he could read the pedestrian arrangements in the sheet music.

I loved being in the barn listening to him play the piano, reading by the fire or talking to other guests. John could accommodate only twenty-four people. Dinners took place in two rooms, with a table for twelve in each. The atmosphere was exactly what it would be if you were a guest at someone's home.

The special atmosphere of Burroughs View Club was once again to be enjoyed by us in Utah, at the Alta Lodge, which was owned, as it turned out, by a Bill Levitt (no relative). Bill followed the same procedure used by Lurie. At mealtime there were no assigned seats. The result was that in several days, strangers quickly became friends. Coincidentally, it turned out that Bill Levitt had also started skiing at Lurie's Burroughs View Club.

Early spring skiing.

1932's Skiing at John Lurie's Burroughs View Club.

In 1972, the social section of *The Sunday Times* ran a lead story about Windham Mountain and a small group of men who had turned it into a private club for skiers with "no lift lines," which was too good to be true. A phone call made it possible for me, and our son Peter to try the club for three days. We quickly gave it our seal of approval. So we became members and for the next eighteen years, Windham, like Westport, added another dimension to our lives.

Mimi and I drove up for a look and found an ideal house with a large living room, a big fireplace, an easily manageable kitchen with an open counter to the dining area, three small bedrooms, and, unfortunately, only one bath. For me, that meant roughing it –Mimi and I had separate bathrooms in New York and in Westport. In Windham, I had to share the bathroom with Peter, Elizabeth, and Clifford Ross who became almost an adopted son after his parents were divorced.

Our house had a comfortable terrace overlooking the valley and the mountain, and we were only two hundred and fifty yards from the main lift. And wonder of wonders, it was an easy two hour and forty-five minute drive, all on a thruway. Our cook prepared four different stews, so that every Saturday we could be our usual six for dinner, the two of us, plus two other couples. If we were invited out, guests would come on Friday night or for Sunday lunch. The ambiance at Windham could not have been more agreeable. The club had been founded by a small group of wealthy Catholics: the Sheridans, the Murrays, the Skaekels, and the Manns. Membership was a mixed bag and always more or less interesting, so we were never at a loss for guests. Skiing at Windham had one big advantage: We were always skiing among friends.

One night, our charming old-fashioned clubhouse caught fire and burned to the ground. A modern clubhouse was built the following year but no one liked it, so a few of the more affluent members built their own clubhouse in the comfortable style of the old one. Now we had a club within a club. Mimi and I and the children went to Windham almost every weekend, plus ten days during Christmas holidays and another week over Washington's Birthday.

I had our fireplace going all day long. Mimi lunched at the club, but I always went home for lunch. When I turned seventy-seven, I began skiing only in the mornings. I loved those afternoons alone, reading with a good fire going in the fireplace and usually listening to the eight-track tapes I recorded from my own large record collection. My recorded tapes consisted of a wide variety of styles. Classical music contrasted with pop or swing, or even a bit of rock just to keep me abreast.

At one point, the club was strapped for cash. Because the dues were too low and the membership was too small, the club was losing money. John Haskell, a friend and a partner at Dillon Reed, headed up the club's finance committee, and he recruited me.

In 1976, I bought the mountain from the club for $1,000. I had to pay the taxes and interest on the mortgage, which was all deductible, meaning a savings, if I remember correctly, of some $600,000. The sale relieved the club of making those payments. The deal was entirely legal and was very helpful to the club, as well as being at very little cost to me. I became the landlord overnight. The club had the right to buy the mountain back in four years. Membership and membership dues increased but they were unable to buy the mountain back, so I turned the entire shebang back to the bank, having no interest in running a skiing center.

Someone that same year (I never found out who), in celebration of my sixty-ninth birthday, painted chair number sixty-nine on the lift gold, with my "Keep Smiling, Mort" insignia up front. Many of the kids waited to ride on the gold chair and many of them started calling me "The Savior," appropriate for a club founded by Catholics.

One morning, eleven years later, as Mimi and I were approaching the main lift, several people greeted me with "Happy Birthday." How could they possibly know it was my birthday? We were on the lift for a minute or two when suddenly I saw a huge banner that ran the entire length of the Carons' porch, adjacent to the lift. It read, "Happy Eightieth Birthday, Mortimer." You can take the boy out of Brooklyn but you can't take Brooklyn out of the boy, so out came, "Holy Cow!" My jaw dropped further as other signs were slowly revealed. Mimi had ordered huge banners printed on some kind of synthetic canvas. There were five Mortimer signs, each supported by two posts. They had to be driven into the frozen ground with a drill. When we got to the top, a second surprise greeted me. Mimi introduced me to Greg, a professional photographer who, with the use of a camcorder, would make a record for posterity of our skiing ability: me at eighty and Mimi at sixty-six. The conditions were excellent, so he was able to catch us skiing at our best.

John Wendly had founded the Seventy-Plus Ski Club. I became a member and earned my membership patch, which gave me the benefit of skiing at a discount nationwide. When I was eighty, I founded the Eighty-Plus Ski Club. I ordered a new batch of patches and sent them to my monogram department. There they changed the seven to an eight, and I sewed the new patches on all my sweaters and parkas. I wrote Wendly a nice letter telling him that I had founded the Eighty-Plus Ski Club but he had no sense of humor. He wrote back that if I didn't stop at once, he was going to bring a lawsuit for infringement. I told him not to worry because I would be the founding, and probably the only member.

I never found Windham boring, more than I can say for the skiing trips we had made to Switzerland– two to Saint Moritz, one to Arosa, and a fourth to Zürs, in Austria. The skiing was so bad in Saint Moritz that first year that we had to take a forty-minute drive through a pass to find snow at another small area that was serviced only by uncomfortable poma-lifts. The skiing there was well worth the drive. It was almost like skiing on the moon. There was a most extraordinary landscape, and a shallow valley at the very top of a mountain provided an intermediate slope. It was seemingly in the middle of nowhere, with no traffic and only a handful of skiers. The landscape had a bit of an eerie quality and during the many times we skied there, there was no sun.

Our two weeks in Zürs were, for me at least, miserable. The hotel could not have been nicer. The clientele was mostly British, although the management did nothing to engender conviviality. As I recall, there was a big lounge with a fireplace but no cocktail party where one might socialize with other guests. There was no sun either and the terrain was too difficult for me. And all of it was above the timberline. Above the timberline means no trees. Without trees and without sunshine there was no perspective, so skiing was dangerous.

To my dismay, I had to ski by myself on what amounted to little more than a golf course slope in the next village. Neither of our children would ski with me in such an ignominious hill, and I was furious. I said that I would never again take them skiing in Europe, and I never did. We all handled it badly; obviously I was just as childish as the children. Sometimes I think I have earned the right to be wrong but in that instance I had not.

Life includes recreation, not necessarily skiing.
Collection of the Author

Of the many mountains we have skied, I found Vail to be the most to my liking, with its trail skiing through the woods. The Village was an updated version of a Swiss village. The mountain was large and there was skiing for every level. On our last trip, however, the elevation of eleven thousand feet was more than I could take. Subsequently, we went to Deer Valley, at a height of nine thousand feet and there we stayed at the new four-star Stein Erikson Lodge.

Deer Valley was earmarked as the first luxury ski area, the first to put boxes of Kleenex on the lift line. They also took off your skis and carried them to and from the lodge or your car. The skiing was relatively easy, and at my age, that was just what I needed. I did not need challenges. I wanted to ski gracefully, with my skis glued together, which, being a dancer, I could do.

Skiing is a wonderful and endlessly interesting sport. It is also expensive, inconvenient, and dictated by conditions of the snow. Inclement weather, from time to time, is to be expected, and we have skied in below zero temperatures punished by blustering winds and even, perish forbid, icy patches. There can also be heavy snow, hail, or even rain. You had to be hearty. However, when one thinks of skiing, one thinks of bright sunny days with beautiful snow and temperatures in the upper twenties without wind. In those conditions, one could ski like a pro. And for me, on those good days, I could ski with the grace of a ballet dancer. Having done it all, we concluded that for us, the club at Windham Mountain was the best. It was cozy, comfortable, nearby, and familiar. It was a home away from home and we all –family and friends – loved it.

13

Mortimer's Restaurant -

Glenn Bernbaum

I was fortunate to find Glenn Bernbaum, the only professional merchant Custom Shop ever had. Bernbaum ran the Custom Shops for twenty years, from 1959 to 1979, as senior vice president and chief operating officer. I had put a three-by-five display ad in *The Sunday Times,* which said in effect, "Wanted: A Presidential Trainee for an Upscale Chain of Men's Stores."

I received some two hundred and fifty resumes and I particularly remember Glenn's and thinking, as I threw his resume away, "Now why would this hack apply for this position?" Glenn had been COO of Franklin Simon, a popular-priced women's store. The following day I received a phone call from a headhunter saying that she had one of the best merchandisers ever, if I could stand a very difficult personality. With such a rave review I said, "Send him along." It turned out to be Glenn Bernbaum.

Glenn quickly established himself as the man I had been missing all those years. His office was at the far end of my building. Mine was at the other end. A hundred and twenty-feet away I could hear him regularly yelling at unlucky members of his staff. Oddly enough, no one ever resigned. Maybe he chose masochists. He never raised his voice with me and we never had any serious disagreement. In fact, when I went to his office, he always stood up and always called me "Mr. Levitt." I succeeded in breaking him of his habit of standing up.

Glenn ran my business like a business for twenty years. In his tenth year, he bought a townhouse on East Fifty-Second Street and filled it mostly with antiques and well-chosen paintings, and every three weeks or so he invited me to his home for lunch. Glenn really knew food. He had a wonderful cook and the variety of dishes he presented at those delicious lunches was "to talk about."

He got along very well with Mimi who one day said to him, "You know, Glenn, there's not a decent place to have lunch in this neighborhood." He said, "I know and I'd love to open up a restaurant with you, but not with Mr. Levitt." And then one day he said to me, "Why do I have to drink in a bar I don't own? Why can't I drink at my own bar? There is a splendid corner available at Lexington Avenue and Seventy-Fifth Street and I'd love to open a restaurant there."

It is a given that a chief operating officer may not have a second business, so it was with my permission that he opened *Mortimer's Restaurant* in 1976. He continued to run Custom Shop part-time for the next three years, coming in from noon to five. I agreed to this arrangement because of my feelings of guilt. Glenn was doing all of the work and I was making most of the money. I had all of the hobbies while Glenn had only three: reading, drinking, and eating good food.

Bernbaum said he would run his restaurant like a club, and that was his angle. His two closest friends were Bill Blass and Kenneth Lane, the jewelry designer. Those two men were at the top of New York's social calendar and their friends became patrons immediately. They came back because the food was good, the prices were low, and the restaurant was relatively exclusive. *Mortimer's* could accommodate only sixty-five diners, and customers were standing three deep at the bar. Under those circumstances, Glenn could afford to be choosy and because he favored only people he liked, his restaurant blossomed like the *Stork Club*, *El Morocco*, and the old *Elaine's*. If Glenn didn't like you, he made it difficult to get a reservation. He was as successful in his way as I was in mine.

It's ironic that I became a mini-celebrity not because of Custom Shop or because of my gallery, but only because many people believed I owned *Mortimer's Restaurant*.

After I sold my Fifth Avenue building, I opened a new office at 18 East Fiftieth Street. We took the entire tenth floor. It was convenient to my flagship store in Rockefeller Center on a Fifth Avenue corner abreast Rockefeller Center's beautiful mall. One afternoon, as I reached the corner of Fifth Avenue and Fiftieth Street, Jerry Schoenfeld, a New York celebrity and chairman of the board of the Shubert's group of theaters, caught me, you might say, face to face.

He literally grabbed my lapels and said, "Do you know what they did to me in your restaurant?" I stammered, "But Jerry, it's not my restaurant." He continued loudly, "I had lunch guests from Hollywood and I reserved a table for three. I was early and the restaurant was almost empty, but they refused to seat me until my guests arrived. When my guests arrived they gave me a table in the rear where waiters were exiting from the kitchen." Schoenfeld was so outraged that such obvious mistreatment could occur to a personality of his stature that he was blind to reason. Finally, he dropped my lapels and continued on his path.

Two week later, Mimi was sitting next to Schoenfeld at an opening and he told her the same story. Mimi said that if Glenn's maitre d' had recognized Schoenfeld for who he was, he would have received the VIP treatment. In large part, however, this high-handed way of handling the public was probably one of the reasons that celebrities flocked to *Mortimer's*. The restaurant was in the gossip columns almost daily.

At the restaurant's pinnacle, *New York Magazine* did a feature story on Glenn Bernbaum and *Mortimer's Restaurant*. The entire cover was taken up with a photograph of the restaurant's interior, with Glenn standing at a table behind two celebrity women guests. The magazine told the whole story of the restaurant's birth and acknowledged the quality food and modest prices, but played up the fact that *Mortimer's* was run like a club and that if you were not a member, meaning one of the favorites, you could not expect courteous treatment. This aspect of the restaurant was overplayed and the result was a backlash. The favorites continued to go, but others shied away and business suffered.

Despite the backlash, Glenn saved *Mortimer's*, and this is how. He started with book parties. *Mortimer's* became a restaurant favored by publishers launching blockbuster publications. The book parties grew into dinner parties for celebrities. Arthur Sulzberger, chairman of *The New York Times*, Henry Kissinger, and a long list of society hostesses fell in line with good reason. Glenn was very creative in redecorating the restaurant to honor the occasion, the recipient, or whatever else he could think of. Giving a party at Mortimer's had a certain caché. *Mortimer's* was beyond parties at the *Waldorf*, or at *Doubles*, or at *Twenty-One*. The personal touch that Glenn added was essential and very expensive. Although Glenn greeted his female regulars with a kiss, he was nevertheless remote; Glenn was a strong personality to whom one could not complain, for fear that they would be told to go elsewhere.

Glenn and I got along famously. Although he lost his temper frequently, it was never directed at me. The two of us had lunch half a dozen times every year, and he was the host. And on more than one occasion, he would have me sample something new that he was thinking of putting on the menu. He also invested money in one or two of my real estate ventures and unfortunately invested offshore with a lawyer he met through me, in a tax deal that turned out sour. It had been too risky for me; I wouldn't go near it.

Mortimer's fame stretched across the seas, beginning with a friend of English nobility. Through him, *Mortimer's* quickly became a must-see restaurant for Europeans and Londoners. Glenn was a homosexual and it is possible that in some way that was also responsible for the restaurant's far reach.

One morning, in September of 2000, Enid Nemy of *The New York Times* telephoned to ask if I knew Glenn had died. Glenn was found dead in his apartment by the maitre d'. Glenn had sold his townhouse and on my advice, bought the building that housed *Mortimer's Restaurant*. He took over the apartment directly above the restaurant for himself. The restaurant had been closed for two days over the Labor Day weekend and when Glen failed to show up the following morning, the maitre d' went up to the apartment and discovered that Glenn had died alone over the weekend. There was no autopsy. Glenn and I had lunched together for more than twenty years, and when he was gone, I realized that we had become friends and I missed him. I still miss him.

14

Real Estate:

My Secret Bonanza

Happenstance: Walter Dessauer's partner in Chrysler Products (women's sports wear) was Murray Rubenstein. Murray's wife, Estelle Rubenstein, was a certified public accountant, a mini-executive, and formerly a right hand to Ralph Jonas, a generous Jewish philanthropist and the former president of Manufacturer's Trust Company. When Jonas was replaced after the 1929 crash, he opened his own business as a wheeler-dealer entrepreneur. Estelle became his right hand and absorbed a lot of his know-how. She had also done some freelance accounting for my Custom Shops.

In 1939, Estelle and her husband, Murray, had accumulated some $250,000 that they wanted to invest in real estate. Estelle explained some of her investment know-how: "Mortimer, an investor <u>never</u> puts all his eggs in one basket." At the time, I had all my eggs in a series of savings and loan accounts. Estelle said, "Mortimer, you really <u>must</u> diversify. Murray and I are turning to real estate. We have $250,000, not really enough to permit diversification. If you would join us with $1 million, we would then have enough capital to limit our risk by diversifying. That would be an advantage for us and also for you because we would not charge you for our leg work."

I said, "It's a deal." Their nest egg was obviously very important to them so they would be giving it their very best attention. By the same token, they would be watching my money because we were in it together.

As the stock market had cleaned me out three times, 1929, 1932, and 1937, Estelle's real estate proposal was a desirable alternate. Real estate became a second business, equal to Custom Shop. In fact, it became a larger and even more profitable business because of tax advantages. Even though my real estate holdings were indeed very profitable, real estate did not given me the pleasure or satisfaction I had from my main business, the Custom Shops. They were something I had created, directed, and owned. In the case of real estate, the deals were brought to me, first by Estelle, several years later by Bill Parkey, a real estate broker who then worked full-time for me, in charge of acquisitions. In 1992, Bill was replaced by Edgar Bohlen. I never saw the buildings we bought or attended a closing. I could not enjoy the pleasure of accomplishment because, unlike my Custom Shops, I made no contribution to our success, excepting for decisions to buy or sell, and then adding additional capital as needed.

All of this had one major advantage beyond gaining the services of Murray and Estelle without charge, and that was the legal tax-free exchange, where we paid no capital gains tax. For example, when we sold a building, I would immediately buy another building which qualified me for a tax-free exchange. The buildings we bought would have one tenant with good credit and a ten- or fifteen-year lease. On average, I have a nine and half-percent return, much of which is not taxable because interest on the mortgage and depreciation are deductible expenses. So, that's what we did. We bought and sold, bought and sold, bought and sold.

In 1954, when Friedy was running the Custom Shops, he showed me a building at 716 Fifth Avenue that he wanted me to buy. A small building, eighteen feet wide, it stood between Harry Winston's building, the world's number one dealer in diamond jewelry, and Rizzoli, the prestigious Italian bookstore. In 1929, that three-story building had been voted the most beautiful small building on Fifth Avenue. It had been occupied by James Robinson Antiques, who sold it to Countess Mara, the expensive necktie company. Overnight, Countess Mara had run into a bad period and could not afford to move in. I bought the building for $312,000. It was to be my flagship store with executive offices above. Some thirty years later, I sold the building for almost $9 million. No brain, no foresight, just happenstance. And so it came to pass that my real estate took a big jump. Like the Custom Shops it has continued to increase and I now own buildings coast to coast.

I had stumbled on a different and incredibly easy way to enjoy a high return without investing in the stock market. The time had come to set up a foundation. Lucky me!

15

Heroin: Synanon

And DaytopVillage

I did not seek to enter the world of drug rehabilitation; it sought me out. It was September of 1963, and we had comfortably settled into our new Westport home. One Saturday night, a friend invited us to a Synanon open house meeting. Synanon was a highly controversial organization that brought a new approach to the problems of rehabilitating heroin addicts. In 1959, Chuck Diedrich, a rehabilitated alcoholic, had opened a modest center for alcoholics in Santa Monica. Though it was based somewhat upon the treatment at Alcoholics Anonymous, Diedrich's approach was quite different. His encounter groups were not like AA's confessionals.

Word of his success spread quickly. So quickly in fact that, unexpectedly, his meetings were overrun by heroin addicts. His treatment appeared to have an almost immediate success due to his "encounter group peer pressure" therapy. In contrast, psychiatric treatment in hospitals had had only minimal success with heroin addicts. Newspaper stories about the wonders of Synanon spread across the nation, and it was as a result of this publicity that a Westport house had been donated. It was Synanon's policy not to locate itself in slum neighborhoods. However, in upscale neighborhoods there was strong opposition by those who did not want their children to live near addicts in treatment. The Westport house became a center of protests.

The meeting Mimi and I attended was fascinating. Synanon's meetings began with a joint recitation of their philosophy. This one was followed by a down-to-earth introduction by Diedrich who was quite charismatic. Diedrich's speech began with the line, "Today is the first day of the rest of your life." The centerpiece of the meeting was the autobiographical story told by two heroin addicts of their rescue from degradation and despair. The confessions were very moving. Coffee and cake wound up the evening, with open discussion among visitors and residents.

Diedrich had flown east to form a volunteer committee that would try to solicit funding from the City. The majority of his heroin addicts were being recruited in New York and their transportation costs to Santa Monica were being paid by Synanon; Chuck thought the New York City administration should chip in to share the cost. I volunteered to join the committee and found myself to be a committee of one. Unbelievably, I was immediately successful. I met with the commissioner who was handling New York's drug problem. Subsequently, he said, in effect, "Sold. I'm in your corner, Mortimer. We are ready to put down a million dollars, with two provisions: Synanon's books have to be open to New York City's accountants, and someone in the city's drug rehabilitation department is to be in constant attendance to keep track of the rehabilitation procedure and evaluate its degree of success." I became a member of Synanon's board with a nebulous title – Director of Public Policy.

The commissioner had pointed out the organization's major flaw. No one had ever shown with cold, hard facts that Synanon was indeed successful in curing heroin addicts. Synanon had never published accurate records on what happened to addicts after they left the program. Both Diedrich's and Synanon's spokespeople were vague, giving in substantiated figures about the organization's "cure rate." Diedrich refused to accept the check-and-balance accounting that New York City wanted. The $1 million would have to be placed on his doorstep unconditionally, otherwise he would not accept the offer. I was distressed when confronted with Chuck's refusal and wrote a long letter to the other board members. The board's response was, in effect, "Diedrich, may he always be in the right, but right or wrong, he is our leader."

Other than Diedrich, the single most important person involved with Synanon was Dan Casriel, a psychoanalyst who spent several months in residence at Synanon and in 1963 wrote a book called *So Fair a House* about his experience. Casriel had studied drug addiction for many years and had treated addicts in private practice. Like almost everyone, he was searching for a method that would be more effective. Casriel's book helped shed light on some of Diedrich's strange, autocratic ways. When Diedrich incorporated Synanon as a tax-free foundation, a board of directors was required that would control the organization. Diedrich explained to Dr. Casriel that an autocratic philosophy was an important part of his ruling concept. "I need as directors dummies I can control," he told Casriel. "I want no one who will be frightened or rebel over what I do – who will be a threat to my authority."

Casriel agreed with this concept of total control at the beginning but he soon had his misgivings about Synanon. Diedrich began speaking of himself in the third person as the all-powerful source. As Diedrich's egocentric talk continued, Casriel decided he had learned enough. Besides, he had completed his book. Diedrich became a dictator and mishandled dissidents. One extreme example came when about twenty years ago, a Los Angeles attorney named Paul Morantz was hospitalized after being bitten by a four-and-a-half-foot rattlesnake that had been deliberately hidden in his mailbox. Three weeks earlier, Morantz had won a $300,000 judgment against Synanon. In the much-publicized snakebite case, Diedrich was charged, convicted, fined, and jailed for his involvement.

While there is no denying that Diedrich launched a revolution in the treatment of heroin addicts with his "peer pressure encounter group therapy," I had come to the realization that Diedrich was running a cult, and I resigned in 1964.

When news of my resignation reached Monsignor Bill O'Brian, president of the World Federation of Therapeutic Communities, O'Brian contacted me about joining his board at Daytop Village, which had been founded by him and Dan Casriel. I joined and very soon became chairman of the board. Daytop was, in effect, a spin-off of Synanon. It was based upon Diedrich's concept, but minus the cult overtones. There was no admission or maintenance charge. Heroin addicts brought before the court heard this sentence: "Either you go to prison or you go to Daytop for rehabilitation."

I had much respect for Casriel's work and for Deidrich's peer pressure therapy. O'Brien was a hard-working, straight-laced, dedicated leader. Daytop hired a high school teacher, Larry Sacharow, to add some cultural education into the rehabilitation process. Sacharow drafted a play with his classes called *The Concept*. It was similar to *Chorus Line* in that at one point each individual stepped up to the front of the stage, telling excerpts from his or her life story. The play simplified the whole rehab process, from entrance to graduation. Cast members were heroin addicts in various stages of recovery. The play moved me to tears and I offered to produce it as an off-Broadway show, with profits, of course, going to Daytop.

I enlisted Arthur Cantor, a friend and theatrical producer, to join me as co-producer. Arthur was a professional and I thought the play deserved the best. I would put up the necessary capital. Arthur wanted to cover only the usual office expenses and his fee as the public relations man, a requisite of the union. *The Concept* opened in 1964. Walter Kerr, *The New York Times*' eminent critic, said, "*The Concept* is the most moving theatrical experience on or off Broadway." The play was a hit. It had a two-year run, a European tour, three showings at the White House, and was subsequently booked at major universities.

Eventually, I also became disenchanted with Daytop because, once again, I could not get accurate figures about the "cure rates." There is no question that Daytop was successful, but (and I'm still only guessing) of every hundred who entered, seventy or eighty dropped out, and we have no way of knowing whether there was any lasting effect. Recovery actually took a full two years in residence. It was a very expensive procedure and the number of graduates was miniscule when compared with the enormous number of high school dropouts (potential delinquents and potential addicts).

Dan Casriel had created his own live-in recovery center. He called it *Arriba*, and it was expensive. He had rented a five-story limestone mansion on East Fifty-First Street, directly across from Saint Patrick's Cathedral. He used the top two floors as a residential treatment center, similar to Daytop, except that these were the children of well-to-do parents who could afford to pay.

Some six months after I began serving on the Daytop board, Dan Casriel approached me and said, "Mortimer, I wear your shirts and I know how good they are, but you have never attended my therapy groups. Please come as my guest." A month or two later, Dan said again, "Mortimer, just come to one session." Finally,

I went. I immediately signed on as a participant and, secretly, as a voyeur. Dan was having considerable success with his groups, based on elements taken from Freud, Synanon's encounter groups (now Daytop's), and primal scream therapy. The groups were, indeed, a revelation and they included, as might be expected, a handful of celebrities.

Toward the end of my first year, Dan said to our group, "It really doesn't pay to bring in a friend. Take Mortimer, for example. He's been with us for a whole year now and he hasn't budged an inch." Subsequently, I participated in an encounter group marathon. A marathon runs for thirty-six hours, with only four hours of sleep. The marathon wears a person out so all defenses are gone. During that marathon, I at one point permitted myself to *feel*. The vow I had taken in 1930, that I would never permit myself to again become so vulnerable, was broken.

After years of experience with both Synanon and Daytop, I came up with a concept I believed would complete the picture. Daytop and other emerging groups such as Phoenix House, did not have the solution to the drug problem, because, as I had long predicted, addiction was becoming worse and worse. That's when I conceived two different ideas: the first was a better way to handle the problem of welfare; the other was a secondary school system to teach social adjustment to socially maladjusted children, a sure way to stop the growth of high school dropouts. These ideas are better spelled out in person, so feel free to contact me for more information. If financing is necessary, that would be no problem.

16

Up to Our Necks

in Culture

For the most part, only the producer makes money in show business. Therefore the backers who risk their money are called "angels." I, and to some extent Mimi, fell into that category. Because of my success in producing *The Concept,* our friend, Rita Frederick Salzman, asked me to become an associate producer of *Dutchman,* a scathing play by the black activist author, Leroy Jones, now known as Amiri Baraka, a Muslim. This melodramatic and shocking dramatization of invisible racial conflict was a hit; it won the Obie Award for best off-Broadway play in 1964.

Dutchman was undeniably intense theater, with fast-paced dialogue between a black man, Al Freeman, and a white woman, Shirley Knight. It all took place while they are sitting next to each other in a moving subway train. The relationship between these two antagonists was raw and the depth of their hatred was revealing.

Our good friend, Michael Brown, had written a new musical, both music and lyrics. The title was *Different Times.* The show had a strong storyline based on an Irving Berlin-type romance: in 1914, a Jewish man of nineteen marries the daughter of a wealthy WASP. He goes off to war not knowing she is pregnant. She dies in childbirth and the boy is raised as a WASP, by his grandfather. He grows up in different times and becomes a senator, never knowing he had a Jewish father. Years later, his daughter brings home a Puerto Rican lover. There was the small cast of seven, plus five musicians, with two show-stopping numbers and easily understood lyrics. It should have been an off-Broadway hit but the reviews were disappointing and we lost all our money. It is a solid evening of musical theater –worthy of a revival.

One summer, the Westport Playhouse put on a new play called *Checking Out*. The play was inspired by the life of Jacob Adler, king of the Yiddish Theater and father of Luther and Stella Adler. In the play, he sends telegrams to his three grown children, saying, "I'm giving a gala party to celebrate my eightieth birthday and I want you there. I have lived my life in style, and after the party, I'm checking out in style." The three children arrive in a tizzy and threaten to commit him if he doesn't agree to have a live-in nurse.

But true to form, Frank Rich, the favored critic for *The New York Times*, killed the show in his review, damming it as "Borscht humor" by citing one very funny off-color joke. Adler, a widower, was fond of bragging about his beautiful wife, how much he loved her, and how much he missed her. Theirs was a wonderful love match; they fought over one thing only: who would take out the garbage? Eventually they resolved that, too. "After making love … she would pick up my penis and let it drop. If it dropped in her direction, she would take out the garbage, and if it dropped in the other direction …"

The following year, the *Queen of Off-Broadway* Lucille Lortel and I produced *Catholic School Girls*. (Lucille died at age ninety-seven.) The play centered on four girls in a Catholic school, from first grade to eighth grade. At a certain moment, each child takes a turn as a nun, and subsequently takes center stage to talk about her life. Some of the dialogue was pretty raw. One girl refused to be a believer. She shocked the audience in her monologue by saying, "If Jesus were here this minute, I'd spit in his face." It is a thought-provoking play with an insider's look at one aspect of Catholicism.

When You Comin' Back, Red Ryder? co-produced with Elliott Martin, showcased half a dozen tourists temporarily marooned in the desert when their bus broke down outside a lone coffee shop. It was a very successful play. Kevin Conway starred in a tension-filled two-act drama that actually had <u>three</u> "second act curtain" moments. The play was made into a film by Marjo, a rock star. The film, based on the play, was so bad it closed before I had a chance to see it.

There's no way to second-guess critics or the audience. Both plays, *Checking Out* and *Catholic School Girls*, had credibility and both held my complete interest. I know I was right, so what happened??

Jeff Coates was the founder of The Manhattan Theater Club. He had been intrigued by London's theatrical clubs and wanted to set one up in New York. In 1972, I was present at a small gathering of potential founders. I became one and was very active. We rented a five-story building on East Seventy-Third Street, having one theater with two hundred and ninety-nine seats as well as three additional rooms, each large enough for an off-off-Broadway theater with about ninety-nine seats. Our first artistic director came from Chicago and brought with him the concept of Chamber Theater; play readings by actors who, in many cases, were members of Equity.

Mimi suggested that I try the same concept in our home with a black-tie evening. The play was to be followed with a delicious sit-down dinner. It was read with actors on stools holding scripts in their hands. The scripts were a ploy since most of the actors insisted on memorizing their lines. The play might have been worthy of two and a half stars, but the evening itself was worthy of four.

Lynne Meadow, a recent graduate of Yale's Drama School, was recruited as our third artistic director, the first two having washed out. I took Lynne to lunch at The Plaza; perhaps she should not have had the second glass of wine. Based on the success of the Chamber Theater evening at our home, I said, "Lynne, our building has one off-Broadway theater plus three rooms suitable for off-off-Broadway. The off-off-Broadway code permits only twelve performances, and that means only four weekends; forty-eight new plays a year. There are not that many new plays worth producing, so why don't we take one room for Chamber Theater and use it to put on plays that my children were too young to have seen. I am talking about works by Tennessee Williams, Eugene O'Neill, William Inge, Clifford Odets, and others of that caliber."

Lynn said, "Mortimer, I'm not interested but if you want to do it and you will subsidize the productions, I'd be very happy and it would add a lot to what we're doing." Sold!

I hired Dan Wilcox as my artistic director (years later Dan produced a two-hour feature film that ended the long-running television series, *MASH*). I gave Dan a list of plays from which he could choose. Two of our most popular shows were Clifford Odets' *Waiting for Lefty* and an English play called *A Day in the Life of Joe Egg*. I established the format. Wilcox would introduce the evening by talking a little about the play and then inviting the audience to stay after the play ends to talk to the director and the cast. You could throw questions or criticism to them.

Here I am at sixty-five.

At the end of our first year, Wilcox was off to Hollywood and as his replacement I hired Barry Moss. Attendance for the Chamber Theater works was frequently larger than the attendance at the shows Lynne was putting on. In all, I put on twenty-one Chamber Theater shows. At the end of our second successful year, Lynne said, "Mortimer, your idea was really very good and now I think the club should take over. I will be the artistic director, so we will no longer need Barry. I hope you will continue to subsidize it."

I said, "But Lynne, Barry has worked very, very hard. He has put in endless hours and actually deserves to be paid more than he has been. I wouldn't think of continuing to subsidize Chamber Theater unless Barry stays on." When Lynne said no, I asked for a meeting with the board's executive committee. I prepared a brief like a lawyer and presented my case. I put my heart and brain into it but the committee turned me down. I didn't understand it at the time but subsequently discovered that Lynne had cosseted a corporation that would make a $15,000 contribution, an enormous contribution in those days. That gave Lynne a new authority, in this instance, to make this unfair move. If I had known then what I know now, that "endless trouble is indeed the price we all must pay for the gift of life, and there are no exceptions," I would have accepted this unfair turn of events with less anguish. Although, I must confess that, thirty years later, history repeated itself at the Levitt Pavilion where I suffered even greater anguish as it hit me (almost as a present, it seemed) for my ninetieth birthday.

Lynne was in; Mortimer was out. She took over Chamber Theater and unexpectedly shelved it when there was no one to underwrite it. Still, it pleases me to know that the concept of Chamber Theater played a pivotal role in the overall development of what the Manhattan Theater Club has become. It continues to appeal to its audience with a wide variety of plays from now successful playwrights such as Terrence McNally, Alan Ayckbourn, Richard Greenberg, Beth Henley, and John Patrick Shanley.

During this period, Mimi had been deeply involved in raising funds for expanding the Town School, the private elementary school Elizabeth and Peter attended. After the children graduated, Mimi moved into "landmarking." She organized the Neighborhood Association to Preserve Fifth Avenue Houses and became its president. She is an active board member of the Friends of the Upper East Side Historic Districts. And Mimi is a long-time board member of the New York Landmarks Conservancy. Unlike me, Mimi gives her all. She is a tireless worker.

During that same time period, and for some twenty-six years, I have been an active board member of the Lincoln Center Film Society. The Film Society is responsible for The New York Film Festival, the kind of event that adds yet another touch of glamour to New York City's image.

Bill Schuman, the brilliant and articulate composer of modern music, was Lincoln Center's president and executive director. In 1972, Bill decided to add film to the arts of Lincoln Center. He recruited my then friend, Marty Segal, to head up the Lincoln Center Film Society's board. Marty asked me to become a board member. Lincoln Center then had ballet, two operas, a symphony orchestra, the chamber music society, the Beaumont Theatre, the Mitzi Newhouse Theatre, and the Film Society. In 1994, jazz was added.

I'm not quite sure how much the film society does for the film industry. Judging by the long list of immature films depicting violence almost at a comic book level and sex almost at a porn level, I have reason to doubt that we have improved the quality level of new films. Nevertheless, the Film Society has the unique ability to honor the great ones at our annual gala benefit.

Marty started it with a bang. Charlie Chaplin, America's world famous expatriate, was living a quiet life in Switzerland with his wife, Oona, Eugene O'Neill's daughter. It was Marty who persuaded Chaplin to come back for a visit and be honored by the Film Society at our first and very glamorous gala. The gala struck the right note and a long list of celebrities was also honored: Clint Eastwood, Elizabeth Taylor, Paul Newman, Laurence Olivier, Audrey Hepburn, Barbara Stanwyck, Sidney Lumet, and so on. These galas sold out consistently, always mobbed by the press, and each benefit added several hundred thousand dollars to lower the Film Society's annual deficit.

Our annual two-week film festival, second only to Cannes, has been an enormous success. In addition, we inaugurated a second festival. "New Films, New Directors" was produced in cooperation with and shown at the Museum of Modern Art (MOMA). And finally, there is an interesting series of programs at the Film Society's Walter Reade Theater. We can indeed say with pride that Lincoln Center's Film Society has made a major contribution to the city's prestige.

One evening, Lincoln Center arranged a social evening so that constituent board members would get to know each other. Charles Wadsworth, the brilliant, witty concert pianist and artistic director of Lincoln Center's Chamber Music Society, introduced me to his wife, Susan. I told Susan how much I enjoyed her husband's humor as he introduced the chamber music concerts and that while I really didn't like chamber music, I did love the piano. Susan is a frustrated concert pianist, which led her to create Young Concert Artists (YCA), which serves as a bridge between aspiring young concert artists and professional management. She invited me to join her board and I said yes. That was almost thirty years ago.

YCA holds annual auditions every January. The finals are held at the Ninety-Second Street Y where a jury of classical musicians selects only those few who, in the opinion of the jury, are sufficiently talented to embark on careers as concert artists. The competition is stiff. One year the jury selected no one. On average, they select between three and seven artists to be managed by YCA until they are taken over by professional management.

Susan is absolutely dedicated to her cause, a wonderful fundraiser and administrator. When I came onboard, YCA was a functioning organization, but very, very small. Board meetings were held in Susan's mother's two-room real estate office. At my first board meeting, we were five altogether and each of us put down our own $2 to pay for the sandwich lunch.

I soon became chairman and Mimi agreed to a series of musical evenings in our home that included sit-down dinners after a fifty-minute recital by young concert artists; mostly pianists, once a quartet, and once a harp and flute duo. The artists are always encouraged to say a few words to introduce their programs, which made for a relaxed evening. As a result of these concerts, I recruited several board members who were in position to make large contributions; foremost was Irene Diamond who contributed over $2,000,000. Irene was a real fan. (*She died in her sleep at age ninety-two.*)

Frayda Lindemann, who holds a doctorate in music, married George Lindemann, a *Fortune Magazine* billionaire who was also a big-time contributor. Equally important, George permitted us to hold our board meetings in his boardroom, one of New York's most luxurious. It occupied the top floor of the

General Motors building, with commanding, breathtaking views of east, north, and west. We could see from river-to-river and when we looked to the east, we were looking onto the 59th Street Bridge, which from that point of view was more beautiful than ever. Our board meetings started at 12:00 noon and ended at 2:00, but the first forty-five minutes were reserved for socializing, eating, and drinking. The sandwiches were absolutely delicious; whatever your taste, it was there along with cold drinks and hot coffee or tea. We ended with fruit salad and cookies. Our board members appreciated having forty-five minutes to socialize.

I was chairman of the board for twenty-six years. When I joined YCA, there were five board members and no endowment. We peaked at thirty-two board members, with an endowment of almost $9 million. Because of my impaired hearing, I resigned in January 2001.

*   *   *   *   *

Twenty years earlier in 1981, while busy as always, I had my first attack of sciatica. I had been under the impression that the pain of sciatica could be eliminated with Sloan's liniment but little did I know. The source of the pain originated in my lower back, a result of overdoing sit-ups in a vain effort to reduce the size of an unwelcome stomach that protruded below the belt. A slipped disk was pressing on the sciatic nerve, evidently the longest nerve in the body. The sciatic nerve runs down the back of the left leg into the left foot, winding up in the big toe. In my case, the pain centered in my left calf and was excruciating, similar to my dentist hitting the nerve in a molar. Aspirin did nothing and Percadan, an addictive drug, gave relief for four hours.

Bob Siffert, my orthopedist, said the only cure was bed rest, so, always wanting to play the angles, I rented a wheelchair. That was the worse thing I could have done. Sitting kept the pressure on the already swollen disk. As the pain got worse, I went back to Bob who called me an idiot and said I would have to be in bed for about seven weeks. He rented a hospital bed and put me in traction. The only way to cure the inflamed disc was to rest it in a horizontal position.

"Oh, here's Mortimer, home from work. Gertrude, put
'Chariots of Fire' on the record-player."
DRAWING BY W. MILLER; © 1982 THE NEW YORKER
MAGAZINE, INC.
A friendly ambiance in the home also calls for music.

When friends telephoned and asked how I was feeling, I was apt to answer, "My cup runneth over." Sometimes I added, "I'm just waiting for the axe to fall." It fell, and I was completely prepared. Luckily it happened on Labor Day, because if it had happened on Memorial Day, it would have ruined my summer.

It seemed unlikely that a person as active as I am could adjust to the inactivity resulting from seven weeks on my back. But I had had so much good luck that some bad luck was long overdue. That thinking permitted me to make the necessary adjustment to the pain, the painkiller, and the lack of mobility. Pain or no pain, I kept quite busy with books, my secretary, and some television, where I discovered opera subtitles for the first time. For me, subtitles were an important discovery because I could now begin to understand why Mimi loved opera. Subtitles made *Der Rosenkavalier* and *Don Giovanni* enjoyable, so much so that I dreamed up a way to use subtitles at the Metropolitan Opera. I wrote a letter to my friend Frank Taplin, who was chairman of the board, saying that I would pay for an experiment with subtitles.

In 1982, there were no subtitles for opera in New York or anywhere else for that matter as far as I knew. Taplin wrote, "Dear Mortimer, How very generous. I'll take it up with my board." I knew that meant into the basket. To my great surprise, he sent me a second letter saying they would like to go ahead and that I should start working with Tony Bliss, who was their managing director. We took the first steps. Tony and I were getting along fine when the door abruptly closed. James Levine, the conductor and artistic director, learned about the experiment with subtitles and said, "If subtitles come in, I go out." There was no further discussion.

I also offered the experiment to the New York State Opera and to the opera in Santa Fe. Both were interested but turned the idea down without seeing anything. Seventeen years later, in 1998, Joe Volpe, the new director at the Met, was experimenting with subtitles on the back of each seat, estimated to cost some $3 million. I sent Joe my former correspondence with Taplin and he invited me to have a personal demonstration. His concept had some advantages, but so did mine.

The subtitles I propose are easier on the eyes, easier to read, and eliminated the up and down head movement necessary with today's titles. However, no one will ever know, because, as of the moment, my titles have never been tried. This is a case where the credentials I lack might have been helpful.

*   *   *   *   *

Reading the foregoing, you might conclude that I was a producer. But in fact, in her own quiet way Mimi was the real producer. When I was sixty-two, Mimi gave me a surprise party at the home of Ellis Ryan at Windham. I couldn't believe that all those nice people were there to help celebrate my birthday.

The enormous sense of independence with which I seem to have been born, did not include the feeling that people would find me, shall I say, lovable. Actually, Mimi gave me a surprise birthday party every year from then on, and here are some of the highlights.

For my sixty-fifth birthday, Edith and Marty Segal gave a surprise party in their home. It was a historic brownstone in Brooklyn Heights, and I was taken completely by surprise. Mimi held my hand when we walked into the house and when the living room door was opened, I realized that these were thirty or so of our friends, and that this was a surprise party. I went white with shock. My Social Security card had been blown up to an enormous two feet by three feet. An artist had been commissioned to make line drawings of my activities (tennis, sailing, piano, skier, stylist, author, etc.) and superimpose a photograph of my face on each drawing. A three-man combo provided music for dancing. We enjoyed a splendid sit-down dinner at four separate tables.

For my seventieth birthday, Mimi arranged a gala evening in our home; a black-tie dinner. The living room was set up theater-style. There were forty-four guests and an elegant dinner served by our own staff (no outside caterers for Mimi). The details of the evening were kept under wraps. The second floor of our townhouse was "off limits," with a special notice posted in the elevator. Together with Manya Starr ("Fifi") and Michael Brown, Mimi produced a show after dinner that was really a "roast."

The performers were our friends: Harold Rome, composer and lyricist; Charles Wadsworth, concert pianist; Norma French, diva of the New York City Opera; Michael Brown, author, producer, performer; Barbara Carroll, my all-time favorite pianist; and Fifi Starr each had a turn. This was followed by a *This Is Your Life* slide show. Mimi had commissioned our long time wonderful friend, the talented caricature artist Al Hirschfeld. (He died in his sleep in January at age ninety-nine, six months short of one hundred). He did a headshot of me, the bowtie gives me away, in case there were any questions. The Hirschfeld was then reduced for the cover of the theatrical *Playbill* program that was given to friends as they took their seats. The title was *An Evening with Mortimer*.

Mimi produced a gala surprise party for my seventy-fifth birthday in a most elegant downtown loft. The owner was a buddy of Leonard Bernstein. There was a rather long show, with some hired help. I had to talk of course; there must have been a hundred and twenty five guests.

My eightieth, eighty-fifth, and ninetieth birthdays were all held at *Mortimer's*. The ninety-fifth (I was going to say, thank God –please forgive) was held in our home. In addition, there was a surprise party for each year in between. Perhaps a word of explanation would be helpful here. Mimi grew up with a life that always included birthday parties. She was sad that up until the time we met, I had had only one birthday party, when I was six. She was moved, knowing how profoundly disturbed I had been celebrating my important twenty-first birthday at home alone, reading Oscar Wilde's, *Picture of Dorian Gray*. Mimi was now compensating. Having said all this, I will not outline every one of those parties but suffice to say, they were gala, and even though the main event was a constant "Me" they were never boring. Perhaps I will outline just one more.

I had suggested to Mimi that we skip my ninetieth birthday because in September I would be celebrating the sixtieth anniversary of Custom Shop and we would also be celebrating the fiftieth anniversary of our marriage. Mimi laughed. "It's much too late. Preparations for your ninetieth birthday party are well underway."

Nevertheless, the ninetieth birthday party was a surprise because I had no idea where it was to be or who would be there. Mimi left me at about 7:00 and our new chauffeur, Paolo, had instructions to wait until 7:30 and drive me to our destination, which turned out to be *Mortimer's*. However, when I walked into *Mortimer's*, the disguise was complete. A huge trompe l'oeil created the impression that we were standing in the front row at *La Scala*, looking back and seeing the grand tier and part of the audience in the orchestra. The effect was incredible because a flat wall was magically curved into *La Scala*, my favorite opera house.

The dinner, as usual, was the chef's gourmet work at its best. And, once again, a thousand roses and balloons covered the entire ceiling. Both of the children spoke and there was a greeting from President Clinton and a Congressional mention, thanks to our friend Congresswoman Carolyn Maloney. There were remarks by friends from every facet of my life.

Mimi worked with her usual two co-producers, Manya Starr (She died suddenly in the summer of 2000) and Michael Brown. There were life-sized photographic cut-out figures, each representing one of my favorite activities. The cut-outs were standing in a row on the bar that had been converted to a stage. Friends were called to make appropriate remarks; Helen Moody (tennis), Jean-Claude Kiely (skiing), Shakespeare (writer), Elsa Maxwell (entertaining), Beau Brummel (fashion), Vladimir Horowitz (piano). After each performance, a caricature of my face was superimposed over the face of the icon.

Ronnie Heyman knows me better than I know myself, and if I ever need reassuring, I re-read her remarks:

Playing tennis with Mortimer is fascinating. But it was never, I'm afraid, about tennis. It was about real estate. Every year, we waited to see what creative arrangements he would make with a court owner who would give up his court every day between 9:00 and 12:00 noon, since Mortimer, like Woody Allen, would never join any club that would accept him. The court could not be hard but neither could it be red clay, which is too messy.

153

Tennis with Mortimer was very much about fashion. I quickly learned that I should wear my best Ellesse for our matches, as Mortimer did not suffer frayed collars or yellowed whites gladly. It was cheaper to buy new outfits every time than to pay a psychiatrist to restore my ego after incurring ML's sartorial wrath. So consequently, I think my clothes were actually newer than the balls we used to use (ever thrifty).

It was about makeup, hairdos, and advice from the Maestro on how to whittle down bulky thighs (you can imagine how fond I was of that topic). But it was always, and I quote, just between us girls.

Mortimer had a system, which was to sit and rest every alternate game, so there was plenty of time for local gossip, financial topics, household anecdotes, and to discuss everything from landscape lighting to the philosophy of life. But we rarely discussed politics, as Mortimer made it plain that he really did not care what transpired in Washington, beyond what sort of shirt the president was wearing.

Out of every hour spent on the court, forty minutes was schmoozing, which was actually perfect, since Mortimer was in his seventies and I had usually just given birth. He was no Bobby Riggs, but then I was not Billy Jean King, and it didn't matter because the whole exercise was really about friendship.

Mortimer had a stable of about thirty of us, the minimum requirement to "feed his habit," since he liked to play every day. And when he was retired, we were busy. I felt he loved his tennis girls, although of course, not in the way he loved one special woman, who just happened to be a golfer.

He was eager to offer free instruction, and if he did give me a compliment on some small improvement, you can be certain it would have been tempered with constructive criticism.

I am totally fascinated by this man, who retired at age thirty-four and went back to work full-time only when he had the time to spare from his other pursuits, who seemed always to have had his wish rather than to wish he had, and who could say outrageous things and generally get away with it.

When he gave up tennis at age eighty-five, Mortimer was only worried that he'd lose those treasured courtside friendships. Nonsense.

Mortimer, being with you is like riding a bike. We can always pick up where we left off, we never forget how, and we never lose that rhythm.

For me, you are a neighbor, a friend, and an inspiration. No matter what the score, ours was always a love match.

Mimi's hand was visible in each of her productions and her talent in this area (I had none, absolutely zero), was repeated in one way or another for every holiday. There was always a dinner party with our children, my brother Ray, and one or two friends, and always some table decoration acknowledging the day. Mimi gave me a birthday party every year, not just the big years, and it was always a surprise. Mimi is wonderful, Mimi is talented, and my appreciation is endless. Life with Mimi continuously renews itself. Hallelujah!

17

The Levitt Pavilion

for the Performing Arts

The Levitt Pavilion for the Performing Arts is a beautifully landscaped amphitheater located on the banks of the historic Saugatuck River in Westport, Connecticut. Residents can come almost every night during the summer for live entertainment, fifty-five nights of music under the stars. Music under the stars, combined with a healthy lawn, is truly magical, and admission is free. There is entertainment for all tastes. One night is reserved for children's programs which start early at 7:00. On other nights we present military bands, concert bands, dance (ballet or Broadway). Friday night, salsa, Saturday night, rock, and Sunday night, jazz. There are several evenings of classical music: recitals, including piano, violin, cello, and once or twice, a string quartet. The number of classical programs depends upon the response of the audience, which is usually poor. Let me repeat that admission is free.

I started the Levitt Pavilion in 1971, and here's how that came about. In 1970, Westport's recreational commissioner, Lou Nistico, wanted to build a bandshell. As originally conceived, it was to be used by unpaid local talent. Nistico had been able to raise only $10,000: $5,000 from the Young Woman's League and $5,000 from the Rotary Club. Winnie Scott, the new director of the Westport Arts Council and a close friend, told me about the failed financing for the bandshell. She said the estimated cost was $40,000 but they only had $10,000. Since our summer life in Westport has been good to me, I said I would gladly give her the rest of the money, providing I approved the Pavilion's design. Going back to my years at Manhattan Beach, I loved listening to music outdoors, especially those afternoons with performances by Harold Stern's modest brass band. Luna Park had its own concert band several times a week. When we were on our honeymoon, I enjoyed listening to music under the stars in amphitheaters, remnants of past centuries in Italy and Greece.

Westport is a New England town on the water, so I thought the structure should be traditional. I turned down the first design because it was too modern. Subsequently, Winnie came to my office, along with Barbara Schadt who was president of the Young Woman's League. Bruce Campbell Graham, a local architect, had designed a stage complete with dressing rooms and a toilet. They brought the plans along and I was happy with them. I said, "Done." They could start immediately. Barbara was responsible, in a sense, for raising the $5,000 that the Young Woman's League contributed to the Pavilion.

I had nothing to do with the construction. The Pavilion is built on a triangular-shaped garbage dump, a peninsula that juts out like an arrow some two hundred feet into the Saugatuck River. The site is twenty-eight feet high and commands a splendid view of the river, the town's new luxurious bridge, and the surrounding area. I was thrilled with the location.

The night of the dedication of the Pavilion was a big event in town. An orchestra concert with a Metropolitan Opera singer and a prize-winning pianist was the program. There was no admission charge since a benefit dinner for one hundred and twenty-five people was organized by Mimi to raise additional money for the Pavilion. When we arrived at the Pavilion, the place was packed: a thrilling sight for us. Our group walked all the way down to the front where chairs had been set up for us. In the welcoming speech, the first selectman announced that the town had decided to call it the Levitt Pavilion and it came as a complete surprise. There was never any discussion about it being named for me.

I have had a long-time interest in lighting, acoustics, presentation, and administration, gained in the sixty years I have owned all those eighty-two Custom Shops. I had very strong feelings about the Pavilion's lack of professionalism. Although I had put up eighty percent of the money to build the Pavilion, and fifty percent of the budget to run the Pavilion all those years, I still had no status, no official position, and was not even a board member. I had only myself to blame. I've earned the right to make mistakes, but my mishandling of the Pavilion was a lulu.

If, at the very beginning, I had asked the mayor to appoint me co-chairman, artistic director, or chairman of the executive committee, the mayor would have. Why wouldn't she? I had been with the Pavilion from the beginning. I was well qualified, having had considerable experience in theater, music, and the arts. But I never asked the Mayor and that was my major mistake.

My authority was tenuous, and over the years, each new chairman thought of me only as a nuisance. My financial contributions were taken for granted, despite the fact that the various chairmen did **not** contribute any money of their own.

In 1994, after an exhaustive interview process, I chose a new executive director who was thrilled. "Mortimer, I can't believe that I'm going to be paid to do that which I enjoy so much and all these years have been doing as a volunteer." Shortly after her appointment, she changed her position. "Mortimer, I take my orders from the chairman, not from you." Although I had recommended the chairman to the first selectman (in Connecticut, the mayor title is first selectman), we had agreed that she would work with me, and would come into New York to lunch with me once a month in the winter. She reneged on that immediately

The new president started the season with $80,000 in the bank and ended $10,000 in debt, a $90,000 loss. She resigned and joined the Young Women's League of Westport. The money I contributed and the money Mimi raised, as a board member took care of half the budget. The balance of cash needed was to be earned by a summer benefit at the Pavilion. That board members had no obligation to make cash contributions was another inexcusable mistake. The major function of a board is to raise the money necessary to run a non-profit foundation. The chairman's battle cry for all non-profit boards is, "Give it, get it, or get out."

None of our other chairmen had adequate background in theater, music, administration, or production. My situation was completely absurd. For example, I have a letter dated 1974 from the selectman stating that I could attend board meetings as a guest, but could not cast a vote. (I was contributing half the budget). On another occasion, a chairman wrote that I could contribute my money but could not tell the board to use part of it for a sprinkler system. Incidentally, an underground sprinkler system, which goes on at midnight, must be monitored several times a week (turned on manually in the daytime for five minutes or so, to make sure none of the lines or sprinkler heads are broken). The system was never monitored, so we frequently had mud puddles and/or drought. We would not know, until it was too late, that the system had been damaged.

The chairman was not satisfied with our life-like sound and spent $30,000, against my objections, on a multi-sound system similar to the one used in Central Park. It was an unnecessary expense, and in my opinion, it substituted canned music (think Yankee Stadium) for what we had, the illusion of hearing the performer rather than the loudspeakers. The chairman also wanted the rock music sound at ninety-five decibels, the result being that residents complained to the police. I had instructed the stage manager not to exceed eighty-five decibels but to my chagrin, he held it down only if I was at the Pavilion.

I was so distressed that I met with Joe Arcudi, our mayor. I said, "Joe, I love the Pavilion but it is costing me too many sleepless nights. I no longer want to be involved. Please, take my name off the Pavilion." He said he would never take my name off, suggested that I stay on, and said that he would give me the authority I should have had all along. He gave me two titles: one as artistic director and the other as chairman of the executive committee. To complete the picture, the chairman resigned.

The next year, I started off with a dream team. Frieda Welch, a longtime board member, became the executive director. Another longtime board member, Evi Allen, became chairman. Because we had worked together very well in the past, I wrote her a letter to say how happy I was with our collaboration:

> *Evi dear,*
>
> *The battles are over. The war has been won, and after twenty-three years I am finally in the happy position of being deeply enthusiastic about the opportunity to work with you and Frieda.*

The fact is, and I have told you this before, I have had many sleepless nights, because, frankly, I was ashamed of the way the Pavilion has been run. I envisioned how it could be, and until this year, that never came close to happening.

The support I am getting from you and Frieda permits me once again to tackle the Pavilion's problems with the same eagerness I had years ago. Happily, the Pavilion is actually giving me pleasure.

So this is just a short note of thanks. "Onward and upward."

Love and Kisses,
Mortimer

In September of 1996, I received a letter from her saying that I was no longer artistic director or chairman of the executive committee. Here is an excerpt, and that letter was sent without the board first passing a motion:

Mortimer,

You are our founder, have been very generous, and have worked hard in support of our success. Indeed, your name graces the Pavilion. You and Mimi are most welcome to continue membership on the board, but you must understand that the board reserves its authority and responsibility to itself. There will be no executive committee, nor will there be an artistic director position. You will have the influence that accrues to being on the board, but, like the rest of us, can have no other authority.

The Levitt Pavilion for the Performing Arts

Sometimes your suggestions will be accepted, sometimes rejected, and the board may decide to move in directions that you think are unwise. All of this is the normal way of such volunteer organizations.

Cordially,
Evi

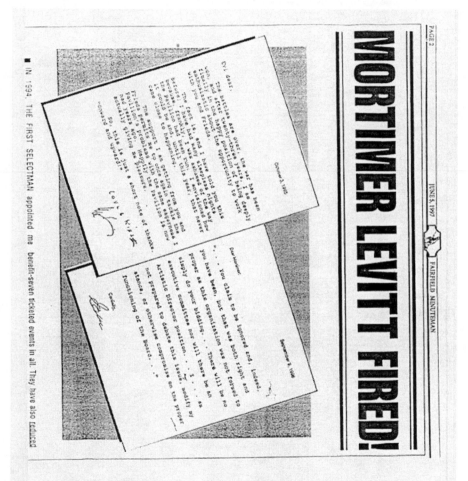

Text of both letters on adjoining pages.

As artistic director, I changed the look of a bare wood stage in several ways. To project a professional image, I chose a new color to repaint the stage. The lighting had always been much too bright, exposing only too clearly the cheapness of our wooden walls. The bare walls are now disguised with soft stage lighting; a pink tint that makes the walls appear to be covered with a rich brown velveteen. Drama was added with three bright spotlights coming down directly from the ceiling at stage center. A new lighting board with a computer chip was installed. I could then tell the stage manager the exact light I wanted, after which he simply pushed a button, and presto, those light settings were recalled.

Further drama was added with two huge comedy/tragedy masks, each six feet long, that I commissioned for the back wall of the stage. Individually focused spotlights were bought to light those masks. A pair of tall green plants were set up, each with its individual spotlight, to add to the stage décor. Five boxes of white flowers were stretched across the front of the stage to create a gala feeling. And finally, white stanchions held up with white chains stretch out parallel to the stage, ten feet in front of it in the grass. Together, the flowers and the stanchions gave the stage a dramatic presence.

Opening the show was a problem. In theater, the lights go down, the curtain goes up, and the show begins. But we had no curtain. I went to a recording studio and created a musical logo that would open every show. At six minutes after show time, the audience heard chimes; a well-known six-note theme, followed by eight gongs that were loud enough to wake the dead. The sounds stopped, the lights went on, and the audience heard, "Once again it is show time at the Levitt!"

In 1995, our twenty-second year, we brought the Pavilion out of its 1994 slump. We tore up the ugly blacktop road that had mistakenly been laid down through the center of our lawn. With the blacktop off, and our sprinklers working, the grass looked like the recently planted blue grass of Central Park's great lawn. And that year, we added theater to the program - five shows originating in off-Broadway theaters - thereby completing our original plan to have something for everyone. With a few exceptions, we were open seven nights a week. Five nights is better because too much of a good thing makes it less attractive.

The Levitt Pavilion for the Performing Arts

So, after twenty-two years of being at odds with various chairmen, I finally had one who enjoyed working with me. Once again, I was looking ahead.

One year after that friendly letter, the chairman and I were at odds. Entertainment at the Levitt Pavilion was always free. But the chairman thought she could enjoy profits by charging admission, so the board would not be required to raise its annual $125,000.

Her first production, an international music and food exhibit, was a Saturday daytime event, whereas everything we do is at night. The event would run from 12:00 noon to 7:00, with six bands playing music from different parts of the world. The admission charge was $10. The event would surely lose money and, if it rained, would be a total disaster. I was and am strongly opposed to charging admission and equally opposed to the food event. However, the board went along with the chairman.

Subsequently, I had a private meeting with the chair and the executive director in an attempt to reach a compromise. I suggested becoming co-chair, and offered to increase my annual contribution to $100,000 in perpetuity. I would also restore the $250,000 bequest in my will. The chairman would create a new board in which each member would be obligated to contribute or raise $1,500 each year. The board would raise $150,000 to match my $100,000. As co-chair, the present person would run the board meetings, buy the acts, and spearhead the fundraising, while I would act as co-chair at the Pavilion, checking the grass, the shrubs, the lighting, the sound, the presentation, etc. By turning this offer down –it would have been a million dollar contribution– the chair and the board denied Fairfield County residents the high quality of entertainment they would have had. If I had become co-chair, we would be spending $130,000 for entertainment instead of the $30,000 to $40,000 usually budgeted.

My offer was flatly turned down even though I had been involved from the very beginning, and I really cared about the Pavilion. Unlike the other board members, I attended the shows frequently. Ironically, this turned out to be, shall I say, a gift from the board, to celebrate my ninetieth birthday.

I decided to take my case to the public and ran a full-page ad in the local newspapers, against the advice of Mimi and our good friend, Fifi Starr. I was wrong and they were right. There was no outcry from the people to reinstall Mortimer Levitt to the Levitt. The public never understood that they were being denied entertainment of a much higher quality. To repeat, this has been terribly upsetting to me, if only because it was so mean and so irresponsible and, finally, so stupid. Who would turn down a million dollar contribution?

That year, 1997, the chairman had bombarded the audience almost every night with requests for contributions and requests to buy tickets to the half dozen admission-charging shows. Our handsome stage was defiled with large advertising banners. The audience, for the first time, was met with a box office. After a further effort to reach a compromise, including several letters and ad hoc board meetings, the new First Selectman refused to interfere. As much as I have written, I am afraid that my readers don't get the whole story. I sent a personal letter to each board member and each letter was addressed personally and sent by first class mail.

The next board meeting was held at the chair's house, a suggestion that I had made. I would have one meeting at my house and other members would also host meetings, thereby lightening the load of the dismal basement office in which meetings were held. Ours was not a good board; members did not contribute or raise the fifteen hundred dollars that was their obligation and there were never enough board members at meetings. We never had a quorum. The long letter that I wrote was never acknowledged at that meeting. I was the founder and major contributor of much-needed funds and was subject to being completely ignored. How could I continue to give money? How could I continue to be such a fool? It was time to resign from the board, regrettably ending my relationship with the Westport Levitt Pavilion.

In my ninetieth year, I sold my Custom Shops and decided to use that money to pay for Levitt Pavilions coast to coast. I offered to pay for the construction of a Levitt Pavilion at Stamford, Conn. and at Fairfield University, Connecticut. The enthusiasm was overwhelming but the elegant Quick Center Board, also on the campus of the Fairfield University, put their foot down. The

Levitt would be raising funds that the Quick Center needed. The University's president sheepishly explained that he could no longer agree to a Levitt Pavilion.

Stamford's mayor invited us twice to luncheons at his club, along with the deputy mayor. However, Malloy wanted the stage taken down at the end of the season. I was contributing $750,000 but not for a flimsy, temporary shell and, at the moment, it's a standoff. Nevertheless, there's more to come, at this time I have offered to pay for twenty-three Levitt Pavilions coast to coast.

This year, two new Levitt Pavilions opened, one in Pasadena, California and one in Harrisburg, Pennsylvania. There are six other Pavilions under discussion: University of Virginia in Charlottesville, Mammoth Mountain, California, SUNY College at Purchase, New York, Oak Grove, Kentucky, Memphis, Tennessee and Lenox, Massachussets, adjacent to *Tanglewood.* The Levitt Pavilion in Pasadena received a large amount of nationwide publicity, which drew the interest of many other cities. I think the same will happen once the Levitt Pavilion in Lenox Mass is in operation. Even though Levitt Pavilions are an attractive asset in every community, there are, unfortunately, political problems to wrestle with.

Our daughter Elizabeth represents the Mortimer Levitt Foundation on the West Coast and has worked closely with the community of Pasadena to open California's first Levitt Pavilion. Elizabeth will oversee all aspects of the Levitt Pavilions when she eventually assumes the role of Foundation Chairman or Co-Chair, thus ensuring the long-term future of our magic; **The magic of music under the stars.** There is no admission charge; it's all free. If it's not too pretentious, I may die thinking that Levitt Pavilions coast to coast will be my legacy, along with *Keep Smiling.*

18

1991, Fifty Years Later,

I'm Back at Custom Shop

In 1979, Tony Bergamo succeeded Glenn Bernbaum as president of Custom Shops. He had recently received his law degree but decided not to pursue a career in law, opting instead for business. Tony was short, stocky rather than fat, and near-sighted, needing thick eyeglasses. He was immaculate to a fault, although he had a sleeping problem. Occasionally at 3:00 or 4:00 in the morning he'd get out of bed and go out for a walk.

Tony was thrilled to make this sudden jump to the top. He was sales-oriented and people-oriented, and generous: flowers, candy, birthday greetings, and over-tipping. One way or another, his presence was always felt. Unfortunately, Tony's generosity may have raised our overhead from seven to fourteen percent.

Although I was standing apart, I knew that a business needs constant watching, and an entrepreneur will always keep trying to make a business better. In May of 1991, after twelve long years, Tony Bergamo and I came to a parting of the ways. I had no replacement, but fortunately Peter Kimmelman, a friend and a financial whiz, became an acting president. Kimmelman was a financial man, not a merchant. He would keep suggested changes to himself: "Don't tell Mr. Levitt." When I inadvertently learned about that the relationship came to an end.

Now I needed another new president. As you can imagine, I had no intention of continuing to run the business full-time. A headhunter in Philadelphia recommended Tom Rheinhart, age thirty-two, with fourteen years of experience at

Burdine's as a merchandiser. I hired him as my new president, but Tom's position came to an end in ten months. Next, a New York headhunter recommended a man who shall remain nameless, with an MBA from Harvard and recently terminated as president of a chain of cutlery stores. That too came to an end in ten months.

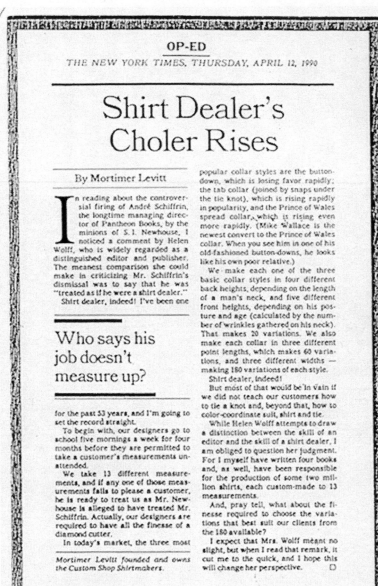

OP-ED

THE NEW YORK TIMES, THURSDAY, APRIL 12, 1990

Shirt Dealer's Choler Rises

By Mortimer Levitt

In reading about the controversial firing of André Schiffrin, the longtime managing director of Pantheon Books, by the minions of S. I. Newhouse, I noticed a comment by Helen Wolff, who is widely regarded as a distinguished editor and publisher. The meanest comparison she could make in criticizing Mr. Schiffrin's dismissal was to say that he was "treated as if he were a shirt dealer."

Shirt dealer, indeed! I've been one

Who says his job doesn't measure up?

for the past 53 years, and I'm going to set the record straight.

To begin with, our designers go to school five mornings a week for four months before they are permitted to take a customer's measurements unattended.

We take 13 different measurements, and if any one of those measurements fails to please a customer, he is ready to treat us as Mr. Newhouse is alleged to have treated Mr. Schiffrin. Actually, our designers are required to have all the finesse of a diamond cutter.

In today's market, the three most

Mortimer Levitt founded and owns the Custom Shop Shirtmakers.

popular collar styles are the button-down, which is losing favor rapidly; the tab collar (joined by snaps under the tie knot), which is rising rapidly in popularity, and the Prince of Wales spread collar, which is rising even more rapidly. (Mike Wallace is the newest convert to the Prince of Wales collar. When you see him in one of his old-fashioned button-downs, he looks like his own poor relative.)

We make each one of the three basic collar styles in four different back heights, depending on the length of a man's neck, and five different front heights, depending on his posture and age (calculated by the number of wrinkles gathered on his neck). That makes 20 variations. We also make each collar in three different point lengths, which makes 60 variations, and three different widths — making 180 variations of each style.

Shirt dealer, indeed!

But most of that would be in vain if we did not teach our customers how to tie a knot and, beyond that, how to color-coordinate suit, shirt and tie.

While Helen Wolff attempts to draw a distinction between the skill of an editor and the skill of a shirt dealer, I am obliged to question her judgment. For I myself have written four books and, as well, have been responsible for the production of some two million shirts, each custom-made to 13 measurements.

And, pray tell, what about the finesse required to choose the variations that best suit our clients from the 180 available?

I expect that Mrs. Wolff meant no slight, but when I read that remark, it cut me to the quick, and I hope this will change her perspective. □

New York Times OP-ED
Thursday, April 12, 1990
Shirt Dealer's Choler Rises
By Mortimer Levitt

In reading about the controversial firing of André Schiffrin, the longtime managing director of Pantheon Books, by the minions of S.I. Newhouse, I noticed a comment by Helen Wolff, who is widely regarded as a distinguished editor and publisher. The meanest comparison she could make in criticizing Mr. Schiffrin's dismissal was to say that he was "treated as if he were a shirt dealer."

Shirt dealer, indeed! I've been one for the past 53 years, and I'm going to set the record straight.

To begin with, our designers go to school five mornings a week for four months before they are permitted to take a customer's measurements unattended.

We take 13 different measurements, and if any one of those measurements fails to please a customer, he is ready to treat us as Mr. Newhouse is alleged to have treated Mr. Schiffrin. Actually, our designers are required to have all the finesse of a diamond cutter.

In today's market, the three most popular collar styles are the buttondown, which is losing favor rapidly; the tab collar (joined by snaps under the tie knot), which is rising rapidly in popularity, and the Prince of Wales spread collar, which is rising even more rapidly. (Mike Wallace is the newest convert to the Prince of Wales collar. When you see him in one of his old-fashioned button-downs, he looks like his own poor relative.)

We make each one of the three basic collar styles in four different back heights, depending on the length of a man's neck, and five different front heights, depending on his posture and age (calculated by the number of wrinkles gathered on his neck). That makes 20 variations. We also make each collar in three different point lengths, which

*makes 60 variations, and three different widths —making 180
variations of each style.*

Shirt dealer indeed!

*But most of that would be in vain if we did not teach
our customers how to tie a knot and, beyond that, how to
color-coordinate suit, shirt and tie.*

*While Helen Wolff attempts to draw distinction
between the skill of an editor to the skill of a shirt dealer, I
am obliged to question her judgment. For I myself have
written four books and, as well, have been responsible for the
production of some two million shirts, each custom-made to
13 measurements.*

*And, pray tell, what about the finesse required to
choose the variations that best suit our clients from the 180
available?*

*I expect that Mrs. Wolff meant no slight, but when I
read that remark it cut me to the quick, and I hope this will
change her perspective.*

*Mortimer Levitt founded and owns the Custom Shop
Shirtmakers*

All in all, in the four-year period of my search for a new president, four
men were engaged – two of our regional directors and two men from
headhunters. Katie Rawdon, my secretary, who had been with me for some
seventeen years, became the chief operating officer. Katie had travel limitations as
a mother of two girls, ages seven and nine. And there were other limitations,
including the fact that Katie had no retail or sales experience. She did not know
the techniques of shirtmaking or tailoring, and she had no experience as a
merchandiser.

However, Katie was bright, well-motivated, and experienced in the sense of
having worked with me for so long. Ironic, as it may be, I had retired in 1941
because I did not want to be a businessman, and now here I was, up to my neck in
business, compelled to play the role. I walked out at thirty-four and was back, fifty
years later, at eighty-four. Katie took charge of administration, while I actively

took charge of training new designers in the techniques of shirtmaking, merchandising, and customer handling. I gave ninety-minute classes once a week, one week to managers and alternate weeks to assistant managers.

I came up with a four-star idea, correcting a mistake that only a beginner like me could have permitted to continue unchanged for almost sixty years. I suggested a new way to handle first-time customers. All these years new customers would be measured by a Custom Shop designer, but Custom Shop was the host. That was the mistake. The customer needed to be taken care of by a shirtmaker, a professional, someone who would be aware of the customer's need and who would end the procedure of taking measurements by saying, "Now, Mr. Customer, I am your shirtmaker. And when the shirts are finished, I will call to set up an appointment. It's important that I am here to make sure you are getting exactly what you wanted. And, God willing, of course, I will be here next year when you are ready to place a reorder." This would boost the ego of the shirtmaker, who would now be recognized as a professional in his own right, not just as an employee.

My failure to change that simple mistake accounts for our ridiculously low reorder rate. It was reasonable to expect a fifty percent reorder rate. We were getting only forty percent, which was totally unsatisfactory. And here is the sad part of this story: My trainers wouldn't, or just couldn't, get our shirtmakers to use this new approach.

I was now working full-time, frustrated at every turn and further burdened by the knowledge that, of my eighty-two Custom Shops, there were twenty-six that I had never even seen. My Custom Shops were not franchised; I owned them all and I was doing them a disservice. At the very least, Katie, even assuming she was qualified, should be out there. But she wasn't and I wasn't. The time had come for me to sell my Custom Shops.

But there was more. Dress-down Fridays had become a normal part of the corporate workweek and, subsequently, casual dress became standard everyday dress in many offices. This turned out to be a disaster for the retail men's wear business; some twenty-five hundred clothing stores went out of business.

I would sell the business, but only with the condition that I be retained as a consultant. POW! I could look ahead to the pleasure of watching the new owner, a bright, young doer, give it his all while I would have the pleasure of sitting back. I'd be a "kibitzer" who would help him avoid the mistakes he was sure to make, not having had the experience of the many mistakes that I had made. And I could now look forward to the next ten years reliving the exciting times I had creating Custom Shop, but I would no longer be a loner. I would be working with someone whose motivation was equal to mine. Cheers! After some seven months of negotiation (I was not present at a single session) I decided to sell Custom Shop to the H.C. Holding Corporation that included Huntington Clothiers, a mail-order business for upscale shirts and ties based in Ohio. Michael Stern was the founder and owner. Mr. Stern would run Custom Shops and Huntington as chairman of both. That was questionable to begin with. Mr. Stern could give Custom Shop only two days a week and Custom Shop, with all its many branches and workers, needed a full-time chairman and a full-time president.

David Yarnell was the moneyman at H.C. Holding. He had a merchandising background at Abraham & Strauss and was a former consultant at McKenzie, a well-known consulting firm. Yarnell was the big boss. He had rounded up a board of investors including Michael Stern who had contributed his company, Huntington Clothiers, to the corporation. It was Yarnell who hired Stern as Custom Shop's chairman. Five months later, Yarnell demoted Stern and installed a new chairman, Chris Fiori, formerly of Coach.

All three men made an assumption that they knew the business and knew exactly what Custom Shop needed, thus deciding that they wanted no input from me. My dream of being a kibitzer was smashed immediately, and that hurt. Mr. Stern moved into Bergamo's office and I sat in my office, completely alone, and totally ignored. There was no consultation. Nothing. We went from the sublime to the ridiculous, evidenced by this excerpt of a letter I received from Stern with the following paragraph in capital letters and bold type:

UNDER NO CIRCUMSTANCES ARE YOU TO EITHER CONTACT OR TALK TO ANY EMPLOYEE OF THIS COMPANY REGARDING COMPANY BUSINESS WITHOUT MY ADVICE, CONSENT, AND DIRECTION. MOREOVER,

UNDER NO CIRCUMSTANCES ARE YOU TO CONTACT OR TALK TO ANY OF THE SHAREHOLDERS OF THIS COMPANY REGARDING COMPANY BUSINESS WITHOUT MY ADVICE, CONSENT OR DIRECTION ...

I WISH TO NOT HAVE YOU PRESENT IN ANY COMPANY STORE WITHOUT MY PRIOR ADVICE, CONSENT, OR DIRECTION.

Now think about this. In the sixty years that I had owned this business, everyone who tried to copy it failed. In sixty years, it's obvious that I must have been doing something right. Yarnell and Stern could never find anybody like me and if they could find someone, they couldn't afford to pay him. They were making catastrophic mistakes without realizing the harm they were doing. I wrote letters to the effect that they were taking the company down the road to bankruptcy.

I continued to be totally ignored and at the end of two years, they were in bankruptcy. Strange as it may seem, I was delighted. I had called the shots.

Subsequently, I was surprised to learn that Tim Bolton, chairman of Express Tailors in Houston, had bought the bankrupt company for, I was told, half its net worth. I could not understand how he could buy the business without talking with me first about the problems. Three months went by before a meeting was arranged, and that was only after I phoned him. The business was being run by three men: all MBA's. They came for lunch and took copious notes, after which there was no follow-up. At the end of one year, their total investment was lost. Stores and factories closed overnight. Several friends who had sold their businesses consoled me. They had had a similar experience, but Custom Shop was unique. There was no other chain like it and these MBAs didn't have the necessary background as shirtmakers to qualify them for running Custom Shop. A sorry end indeed.

19

Ninety-Six and

Too Busy to Die

And what is making me so busy at my age? It's my aptitude for creating solutions to political problems: city, state, and federal; plus, an effort to contribute some twenty Levitt Pavilions in communities coast to coast.

Unfortunately, my dream of becoming the consultant at Custom Shop never came to pass. Fortunately, I could look ahead to creating new Levitt Pavilions, using the money that I had received from the sale of my business. Obviously, I have a large correspondence with the various mayors. I often have them and their deputies for lunch and subsequently there are the additional meetings. I am also putting the finishing touches to the manuscript for this book.

Oh, if that were all. Aside from the book and the Levitt Pavilions, I am still an active board member at Lincoln Center Film Society and Chairman Emeritus, at Young Concert Artists –still active. In the last two years, I have written a syllabus for three different lecture courses, two for colleges and a third for a group of Long Island high schools.

At an annual Bard College benefit, Leon Botstein, Bard's literate and prolific president, who is also conductor of the American Symphony, complained that the audience for classical music was shrinking although the number caught sleeping may have been increasing. As I have been involved with music for so many years, I started wondering what could be done. I came up with a lecture course that would create a group of qualified "Musical Ambassadors," men and women who would act as hosts for classical concerts. If the idea worked, there would be hosts in Carnegie Hall, Avery Fisher Hall, and in most of the musical auditoriums from coast to coast. The best way to explain it is to read the warm welcome concert-goers would be getting from the auditorium's host, their *Musical Ambassador*. These remarks might vary from concert to concert but the underlying theme would be the same. The following four hundred and ninety-six words were revised many, many times:

A Warm Welcome

Ladies and Gentlemen – I have been a teacher so long, I almost said boys and girls – my name is Katherine McQuiston; friends call me Kate. McQuiston is neither Irish nor Scottish, so I will need you to take me at face value. I have been engaged by the board of directors of Carnegie Hall to act, shall I say, as a musical ambassador –a pretentious way of saying, your host. Our hope is to create a more congenial environment for those good people who still listen to classical music. For those of you who do not frequently come to concerts, the atmosphere can be intimidating and we would love to change that. We are here to enjoy a delicious, distinguished evening (afternoon) of classical music.

Now, the idea of having a host was no sudden whim. My professionalism, aside from my degrees in musicology, was honed specifically at Bard College to help make our musical evenings more enjoyable. Now, just between the two of us, the size of the audience for classical music has been shrinking, but the number caught sleeping has been increasing. My function is to increase the size of the audience – by asking your help. If this is a commercial, it is indeed for a worthwhile cause.

You undoubtedly know that most operas come with a prelude, and Broadway musicals come with an overture, the purpose of which is to acquaint the audience with some of the music they're going to hear so that when they hear it in the body of the work, it is already familiar, making the music more accessible. I believe most of you will agree that listening to music you know, is more enjoyable than listening to music you don't know.

And this is the second part of my job: to give you, shall I say, not a prelude, not an overture, but what you might think of as a skewed attempt to put the two together by offering something which has not previously existed. And to do this, we need your indulgence. As this is a subscription audience, it means most of you are sophisticated and knowledgeable; you know the ins and outs of classical music. However, for each one of you who is so blessed, there may be two or three less sophisticated, and they really need your indulgence.

All of you will hear the music, but only the lucky ones will be listening. However, I will give everybody something to listen for and that will make the composer, the conductor, and the musicians happier.

If you have any questions about the composer, about when this was composed, if there is something, anything you want to know, you will find the answers on page fourteen of your program. My job is to give you something to listen for and I will play the opening theme for which you will listen, knowing that the theme will shift from slow andante to fast allegro, possibly from major to minor and in a symphony, from violins to brass, from brass to cellos and bass and from bass to the French horns and clarinet and wind instrument. So with all that said, it's time for me to get to work.

At this point, our host goes to the piano and says, "I will play the theme for the first movement and this is what you will be listening for... after intermission, I'll be giving you a theme from the second half."

The syllabus required a period of meetings for almost one year and the whole procedure was auditioned for six of our friends, all of whom are ardent concert goers. As I suspected, they were indeed hostile at the beginning, but by the end, all six agreed that this would make classical concerts more enjoyable for everyone. And, may I add, long overdue. For a symphony, the themes will be played on a viola; if the host can't play the viola, he will use a viola player from the orchestra. If the host can't play the piano, someone who does will play the theme.

I was lucky to have made the acquaintance of Kate McQuestin, a Columbia University professor who teaches the history of music. She loves the concept and acknowledges the audience's need. Bard College accepted it with considerable enthusiasm. Unfortunately, Kate found out that she had a long term illness and had to resign. I hope that the course will start in 2004.

* * * * *

I wrote a completely different music course to seduce high school freshmen, permitting them to enjoy music other than rock, rap, and disco: a wide range of music which to them is like Greek to me. The title, "An Insider's Look at Music –From Rock to Bach and Everything in Between." I was lucky to have met Gary Schall, the musical director of five high schools in Long Island. He was desperate, fighting an uphill battle to get music into the schools, and this was again a hand-and-glove fit. That course will also be starting in the fall.

* * * * *

My friend Walter Anderson, publisher of *Parade* magazine, introduced me to Mercy College. I had lunch with the president and suggested a fellowship, open only to women students, and of course, I would subsidize it. The school agreed and would permit me to interview the two nominees. I had no authority to vote, or even to indicate my preference, but in talking to these girls over the years, I had come to realize that for the most part, college freshmen are turned on by sex, beer, sports, and an ethereal sense of freedom from parental control. Evidently, only one or two percent are scholars (impatiently dismissed as nerds), their aptitudes having already kicked in. So then, how to motivate these unmotivated students? I came up with a concept for a lecture course for Mercy College freshmen. Lucy Lapovski, Mercy's President, loved the idea.

The title: "Civilization: The View from a Satellite." My course has now been in use for the past three semesters. During that time, in succession, I worked with one teacher and two professors but I decided I had to write the whole thing myself. The best way to explain it is to let you read a clip from the opening lesson:

So, ladies and gentlemen, is there anybody here who knows what they want to be when they grow up? I'll amend that to say, has anyone here decided what he or she will do after they graduate? Please raise your hands. I see two hands. You may be relieved to know that that's a normal response. Incidentally, those few who know, or think they know, what they want to do, are off to a good start. If, perchance, you are one of those blessed with an aptitude – an aptitude is an inner scream that says, "I want to write!" "I want to paint!" "I want to teach!" "I want to be a detective!" "I want to be a tennis champ!" "I want to be a surgeon!" and so on – then you are one of the lucky ones.

Each one of you has an aptitude, and we will try to uncover those aptitudes so that you can more productively select your electives. Once you recognize your aptitude, you are automatically pointed in the right direction. At the very least, ladies and gentlemen, this should start you on the way to your future.

In any case, my name is Tom Willis, which raises another question – are you going to call me "Mr. Willis," "Professor Willis," or "Tom?" I would like to suggest "Tom," but, at this point, perhaps we should show some respect for our college. Maybe we should try "Professor." That is unless I fall apart and dissolve before your very eyes. Bottom line: respect must be earned. I'd like a moment to repeat the purpose of this class is to give you perspective, a perspective that will enlarge the horizons of the environment into which you were born. But most importantly, the objective is to dig out those aptitudes – your personal aptitude – so that, given this overall perspective, you will then be better qualified to select electives, and hopefully you will have been turned on by one of the disciplines that we will look at. Should you say to yourself, "Gee, I didn't know that," it may be your aptitude that's kicking in. You want to know more? Maybe, you are motivated.

The first problem we handle is something near and dear to the heart of everyone in this room and that is your inevitable death. Man has a primal need to survive and the problem of death has been resolved by religion. Almost all religions promise eternal life; so much for the "death" problem. Unfortunately, Jehova does not promise eternal life, so, once again the poor Jews are getting it in the neck.

The course gives the students an overview of fifteen or twenty disciplines covering some things they never knew. The course does enlarge their horizon and if the student's interest is sparked, he is in our corner.

* * * * * *

What else keeps me busy? Years and years ago, I resigned as chairman of Daytop Village because I realized that the demand was greater than the supply; that the number cured was pitifully small when compared to the number that needed curing. That number was increasing because our elementary schools and our high schools were failing. The teachers were faulted, incorrectly, I believe. Socially maladjusted children were being raised in the homes of socially maladjusted parents. They were growing up in a socially maladjusted ambiance that made teaching impossible. Students coming to school with knives, guns, and drugs caused a moral flip-flop, and school was a nuisance they approached without respect.

As the problem could not be handled inside the home, it had to be handled outside. I came up with an idea for a second school system, a school to teach social adjustment. However, it would not be called a school and it would not be seen as one. It is peer pressure therapy with a deceiving title – Tiger Woods Social Club, Derrick Jeter Athletic Club, Lisa Lobos West Side Social Club, whatever. It is an inexpensive way to arrest the escalation of juvenile delinquency.

* * * * * *

Just as the problem with drugs had escalated, so has the problem of welfare. I have come up with a relatively conservative but constructive way to handle that problem. In Israel, a similar problem was handled with the Kibutzim. Anyone needing welfare would be transferred to a Kibutz where they'd be bedded, clothed, and fed. Parents would work five days a week and their children were educated in a school learning a trade or a skill.

Continued stimulation would result from encounter groups twice a week. Peer group therapy gives voice to the voiceless. I have never had time to seriously pursue either of these concepts but I believe that one day they will be uncovered and attempted. In the sixty-five years that I have become aware of these problems, they have not improved. On the contrary, they have become worse and I am still searching for someone who might be in the position to take on one of these concepts or, at least, to take the next step.

20

Old Age and

Even Happier? Yes!

I've figured out that I have, at most, another eight years to live. I can't believe there are so few years left because life has always been forever. My paternal grandfather lived to be ninety-four and he was a heavy smoker. I have had a better life. Theoretically, I should be able to outlive him by ten years. I'm still looking ahead to the gala openings of all those new Levitt Pavilions. And that will be it, ninety-six plus eight; a hundred and four, and out.

The progress of aging is almost invisible, but relentless. One morning when I was combing my hair, I discovered, shocked I must say, that the hairline above my left eyebrow had thinned out, it seemed, without my having seen it. My barber suggested using a hair gel. Magic! The secret of using hair gel is not to leave the stiff look, but to comb it out after the gel dries. Actually, I am still receiving compliments on my full head of hair, but the process of losing hair was absolutely invisible. Occasionally, maybe once a week, there was one hair in the sink bowl. Ironically, the next morning there were three hairs in the sink bowl. I'm not kidding. After that, a lone hair has been there almost every other day and now I have come to realize that all together my hair has thinned out, and it won't be long before that is visible for everybody to see.

The loss of sports moved more quickly: eighty-five for skiing, eighty-six for tennis, eighty-seven for sailing my boat alone. And once you hit ninety (for some people, I guess, eighty), the changes pick up speed. I'll give you some examples, but not necessarily in sequence. My neurologist found a neuroma in my left ear. A neuroma is a common type of benign tumor, which in my case has affected my balance. If I don't look down when I walk, I will occasionally lose my balance, and it is only a matter of time before I start using a cane. Despite the cane, I will undoubtedly join the thousands of seniors before me who have suffered a broken hip because of that long expected fall.

I'm beginning to think of myself as Mortimer Dropsy. In the morning, I take some six pills and use soap, toothpaste, water for gargling, a comb, and a brush. Every morning, I drop one or two things when I try to pick them up to use, and there you have it: Mortimer Dropsy. Not a serious problem, but a nuisance. In the summer of 2000, at a Brooks Jones' lunch party in Westport, I tripped over a Persian rug and got up with a three-inch flesh wound in my left arm, spurting blood almost like water. A knowledgeable guest said, "You must go immediately to the emergency doctor on the Post Road. You will need stitches." Fourteen exactly.

Two weeks later, leaving the local landscaper, there was an inch and a half drop from his path to the sidewalk. I didn't see it and fell in full view of all those automobiles rushing by. It was a most humiliating experience that brought me right back to the emergency doctor. Twelve stitches. I'm not including the five or six times I bruised one of my legs with my new, expensive and very heavy attaché case, evidently designed to maim a mugger.

In the summer of 2001, my tumbles started with a dinner party on a lawn under a tent in Ridgefield: cocktails, some classical music, then dinner and dancing. At one point, I wanted to get up and pushed my chair back, but it stuck in the grass. The chair and I together fell backwards. Why I didn't hurt my back or my head I can't explain, but we had to leave the party immediately because there was so much blood on my right leg, just under the knee. It was almost midnight when we reached Norwalk Hospital. Twenty-four stitches. The staff was considerate although we did not get home until 4:00 in the morning.

Fortunately, I haven't lost my sense of humor and I needed it, because the next morning I put a gash in my left thigh, a story that is too complicated to explain. This lead to another visit to the Post Road emergency doctor and twelve stitches. At the moment, I have various wounds: two on my left leg, one on my left thigh, one on my right knee, another on my right calf, and another on my right wrist. I'm bandaged up like Charlie Chaplin in one of his earlier films. And I'm leaving out the bruises that occur when I walk through a doorway and bruise one of my sides. Still smiling? Of course. It's small price to pay for being alive.

Recently, I've read several books and half a dozen articles dealing with the problems of aging, none of which echoed my experience. The fact is that as I got older, my life became better and better, right up to my ninety-second year, when it abruptly soured. That was when, unexpectedly, my hearing became bad enough to be more than a nuisance. My hearing has dropped precipitously. I used to be able to talk with Mimi at dinnertime even when I forgot my hearing aids, but no more.

The whole process was very slow, and then one day I discovered that the music I was hearing when playing the piano was no longer the music I had enjoyed. My playing hadn't changed but my hearing had changed so it no longer sounded the same. The same went for the sound of music on my CD's. Music has ceased being part of my life and another one of my senses gone.

I've cut down on movies and theater, substituting with closed captioned (sub titles) rental videos. Television sets are now required to show subtitles, which are frequently included with news programs. So, by the skin of my teeth, I'm getting by. Along with *The New York Times*, I keep current. I regret to tell you that I must remove my hearing aids to speak on the telephone because of feedback. Most of the time, I receive calls on my cordless phone. I finish the conversation and walk away, inadvertently leaving my hearing aids behind. It happens time and again, almost every day. In addition, I remove <u>both</u> hearing aids to put on headphones for watching television. When I stop watching, once again, I leave those hearing aids behind. It is very frustrating, almost amusing; finding the misplaced hearing aids has been taken on, as a personal challenge, by Mimi. Lucky me! Mimi is a four-star finder, exactly what I need. On the other hand, should it come to pass, it gives her sufficient grounds for a divorce.

The Burt Mannings (Lynn is a sex therapist, Burt was chairman and COO of J. Walter Thompson) invited us to dinner at their Stamford, Connecticut home. It was a dinner party for ten, all at one table. Two of the guests were exceptionally witty and there was endless laughter, but I, who have always been part of creating that laughter, was silent. There I sat stone-faced, so unlike me, an outsider because I could not understand a single word. The jokes all passed me by. That really hit me hard because as far as I could see, there was no way around this problem, and for me it was kind of tragic. After dinner, Lynn, seeing my pain, suggested a surgical implant. I made an appointment with the surgeon she recommended. Unfortunately, it wouldn't work for me. I am now obliged to refuse most of these invitations.

The acoustics in our two dining rooms are heavenly because long ago I installed acoustical ceilings. We no longer have six for dinner. I've reduced it to four and made the dining room table smaller, so we can happily still "practice the gentle art of conversation" at our intimate dinner parties.

I believe you should also know that my memory problem has become more than a nuisance. Like my friends, I occasionally forgot names, but now it happens five or six times a day. Fortunately, it has not yet affected my thinking: this book is evidence that I'm still all there. However, I seldom leave a room without having to go back for something left behind – eyeglasses, hearing aids, my briefcase, a book, the newspaper, an umbrella, a package. I forget a phone call, to leave a message with the cook or butler – it's another nuisance, a chronic nuisance. Yet, it's a small price to pay for the wonder of being alive.

Not so amusing is the fact that I'm always cold. To be specific, indoors the thermometer has to read eighty-one degrees. In our office, girls in their blouses were comfortable at seventy-two degrees; I would have been chilled to the bone. And despite the endless compliments about how elegant I am, I'm surprised to find people consistently jumping up to help me; opening a door, permitting me to go first, walking me to the door, helping me down the outside steps, giving me their seat on the bus, and so forth.

Not so incidentally, the fact that I do not enjoy walking has resulted in an unexpected and unwanted change. Because I don't take walks, the muscles in my legs have almost atrophied, so the best I can do today is to walk around one square city block. That means shopping is almost out of the question. Museums work okay because I get a wheelchair and Tony pushes me around. On the other hand, several friends younger than I walk with a cane, and some of them use the elevator instead of walking the one flight to our library. Happily, I can still walk that one flight and in Westport I do it five or six times a day because the master suite is one flight up and there is no elevator.

On the other hand, in the last two years, seven women, all strangers, kissed me. They actually kissed me. I thought it was due to my charming personality. Mimi pointed out, and she was so right, that it was mainly because I was old, and possibly, she added, because I was personable, witty, and "snappy" with my bow ties. Subconsciously, perhaps, I was a role model for those who hungered for the longer, more active life I was living.

Writing sessions are always limited to three hours. Otherwise, my brain sends me a message: "Don't overdo it!" A friend who read my manuscript before it was published was puzzled. "Mortimer, how can you be looking ahead when it must be obvious, even to you, that you must be deteriorating?" "Because," I responded, "I am living through these changes. It's my show, it fascinates me, and I have neither cancer nor AIDS." Watching a friend's deterioration is not fascinating, but my own deterioration is, because I'm the only one who can see it through my eyes. How does one find answers to life's questions? You don't find them. You live them.

21

Keep Smiling

On the first of April in 1998, April Fools Day, I received the first warning of my mortality. After chairing that day's Young Concert Artists board meeting held, as usual, in George Lindemann's boardroom on the top floor of the General Motors building, I walked down Fifth Avenue to keep a 2:30 appointment with Alex, my barber, at Fifty-Fourth Street. I was halfway down that block when I started wavering badly enough to stop and lean against the building, and badly enough for a young woman to overtake me with, "May I help you, sir? You seem to be having trouble." I said, "I better get a taxi, even though my office is only four blocks away. Please help me to the curb and I'll hail one."

I was shocked to discover that I couldn't move my left leg. A man joined the woman and between them they carried me into the lobby. They sat me on a chair and the concierge called my secretary, instructing her to cancel my barber's appointment. Then he called my wife who unexpectedly was home. In answer to these kind humanitarians, I said, "I'm having a stroke." My left foot now seemed to be made of lead and there was a ripple effect in my left arm. I wanted to insert my left hearing aid but my fingers missed the area by an inch.

Mimi hot-footed down Fifth Avenue with Paolo. Paolo and the concierge carried me to the car and we headed directly for the New York Hospital Emergency Room. Having been at that hospital several times, I was quite comfortable and felt completely at home.

My blood pressure, which has always been low to normal at one hundred and thirty, suddenly shot up to two hundred and ten. The intern put me through the usual tests and when my neurologist, Dr. John Caronna, read the results, I was given two medications. One was to further thin my blood and make it less likely for me to get another blood clot (stroke), while the other was to bring down the high blood pressure. Then I was given an echocardiogram, and was to be scheduled for an MRI. The MRI test would reveal what happened to my brain.

Incidentally, seven hours after the stroke began, while I was still in the emergency room, the symptoms disappeared. We were having dinner guests Saturday night and this was Wednesday, so I wanted to get out of the hospital in time. But Dr. Caronna needed to know why my stroke had occurred, the reason for an MRI. I became quite tense when I tried to schedule an appointment for the next day. The MRI people refused to give me the requested appointment with no explanation other than that they would try. The next day, the MRI people dragged me out of my room in the middle of my lunch. I should say they wheeled me down on a rolling bed. I had had an MRI several years ago because of my neuroma, and the experience was a little frightening. They strap you down, body and head, and wheel you into a tunnel. You can't move and are surrounded by walls so close to your body that the effect is almost like being buried alive, to which, and I'm not joking, I had a bad reaction likened to panic.

I had been able to handle the prior MRI test because a slim mirror installed above my forehead permitted me to see the operator. He could talk to me and I could talk to him. But when they put me into the tunnel this time, there was no mirror, and that was very frightening.

Anyway, when I got inside the machine and there was no mirror, I said to myself, "Why should I suffer their incompetence. I won't." I yelled, "Get me out of here! I won't stay!" I yelled at the top of my voice like a child, worried that they might not be able to hear me, seemingly being so far away.

These had been two tension-filled days and nights. The first night my IV machine stopped working three times and the loud beeping woke me each time. Three times a technician had a shot at fixing it without success. Finally, I made a suggestion that fixed it, giving me the pleasure of saying to myself, "Oh, Mr. Levitt you are so smart."

Every cloud has a silver lining. My right hand had formerly been trembling so badly I spilled soup all over myself at a UN luncheon. The stroke moved the tremor from my right hand to my left hand, so I no longer had any trouble drinking soup or holding a coffee cup.

It took me a long while to understand that, in general, misery, loneliness, sickness, financial reverses, malicious gossip, shabby treatment by friends, the misfortune of children, and the duplicity of lovers are a normal part of every life and should be expected to continue with varying degrees of severity. "A variety of troubles is indeed the price we all must pay for the gift of life, and there are no exceptions. There are no exceptions."

In childhood, we are led to believe that young lovers marry and live happily ever after. As adults, we probably never quite get that idea out of our head. As a result, every disappointment or misfortune may be felt as an unjustified and personal kick in the pants. But mishaps are the norm and crisis is commonplace. As E.B. White wrote, "Life is choked with laughter and choked with pain." Accept your problems for what they are, an integral part of life's pattern, because life itself then becomes more serene.

Metropolitan Museum Gala

If your personal problems become overwhelming, you can put them into better perspective by involving yourself in group therapy. Your problems become easier to handle when you realize that a group of completely normal, gainfully employed adults have problems that are just as severe, unsettling, or annoying as yours.

Even if you don't need the therapy, you may want to consider joining a group for the additional insights it will give you into the realities and complexities of living. We have one friend, a very successful attorney, who believes that anyone who can afford it should visit a psychiatrist once a week in the same way that an ardent golfer might take a golf lesson with his pro once a week. (Not recommended.)

From time to time, I have received letters from customers who, for one reason or another, were disappointed with our service. However, their distress couldn't be expressed more passionately if their indigestion had been diagnosed as cancer of the stomach. If a man's shirt problem is perceived as a tragedy, you may well imagine what the rest of his life is like. Such a man (in one way or another, they are legion) has lost perspective. He is miserable with himself and miserable to be with.

I had my own unhappy experiences with a classic seven passenger Rolls-Royce limousine in 1957. It was so beautiful, with running boards and those huge headlights. I could sit in the back of my Rolls with my hat on, as the window separating me from the chauffeur went up and down with the push of a button; communication was easy with an interior telephone. But that car was endless trouble because the service was impossible and the charges beyond belief.

So I learned that, regardless of label, one deals in the final analysis with people, and error is inevitable. I learned to roll with the punches, remembering Gracie Allen's advice to take "the bitter with the better." Dealing with adversity, real adversity, actually makes one stronger. There is a sense of accomplishment after one has handled an unhappy experience with grace.

Think about this. Should you be burdened with one of life's more serious problems, do not permit yourself to fall into a state of helplessness. Those who get the most out of life will marshal their energy and wits to fight their way through. Being prepared for disappointments permits one to handle them with a minimum of trauma. Lady Mendel's well-known quote, "Never complain, never explain," states it one way. I say it another way with the phrase used to end my personal letters: "Keep smiling."

Katharine Hepburn, in her seventies, reached a similar conclusion. "I've had certain things happen to me," she said in an interview, "that I was unable to view with a sense of humor at first, but I have struggled through and discovered that the remarkable people I've known just seem to have that knack of being able to see things with a sense of humor. No matter what they are. It's part of our age. I think we're finally at a point where we've learned to see death with a sense of humor. I have to. When you're my age, it's like you're a car; first a tire blows, and you get that fixed, then a headlight goes, and you get that fixed. And then one day, you drive into a shop, and the man says, 'Sorry, they don't make those parts anymore."

Each life has hundreds of unpleasant moments, some trivial, some tragic. How you handle these bad moments determines, to a great degree, your state of mind. You may handle life with equanimity or fall apart with self-pity. Here are two examples:

It has been sixty-three years since I met my first wife and we remained friends throughout her life. Annie Shore had enormous energy, a steadfast belief in the soul of man, and fortunately a sense of humor. But 1978 proved to be cataclysmic. She was mugged twice, the second time suffering a broken leg. In March she was told she had lung cancer, and in April she underwent the necessary surgery.

Keep Smiling

Annie's Christmas card for 1978 included a series of cartoons illustrating a resume of that year in verse:

Ninety-Six and Too Busy to Die

I've given the gate to '78.
There's hardly a date
I didn't hate in '78.

End faster, faster
I wished of that disaster.

But wait--
One more look at '78.

Thanks to friends who in the clutches
Helped speed the end of stinking crutches.

And listened while I sought to answer
Of how the hell
You cope with cancer.

And all that time the world keeps going,
Revolutions ebbing, flowing

From Michigan, T oCarolina
Folks welcome recognizing China,

Want an end to Shahs and Boers,

Seek peace and freedom,
No more Wars.

The jinx is past, I'm feeling fine
A toast to the promise of '79.

SHORE'S SAGE, 1978

Keep Smiling

Women seem to handle adversity better than men. I know five or six women who were widowed, and three whose husbands left to marry someone younger. In each case, the unfortunate woman came out fighting, had an immediate makeover, with new clothes, a new hairdo, and new activities. In contrast, the men whose wives walked out (four of them to a lesbian relationship) broke down in tears.

Jim Segal handled cancer in his own way. Mimi and I met Jim and his lovely Japanese wife, Yo Yo, in Morocco. We became fast friends though the Segals are twenty-five years younger. Jim had a brilliantly successful career with Grey advertising agency. He invested his savings in New Jersey real estate, made a bundle, and decided to go into partial retirement with Yo Yo and their two children on a large farm in the northern Catskills. It was there that he was struck down without warning by terminal cancer. He and Yo Yo dropped out of sight and he refused to let us visit. Eighteen months later, a very special letter arrived, reproduced in part below, which explained their disappearance.

Dear Mimi and Mortimer,

Yes, the news of my death was premature. My demise, planned for September of 1977, did not come off nearly as well as scheduled, to the not inconsiderable annoyance of my doctors. So no, I am not in heaven, I'm inHouston, where Yo Yo and I are alive and well and crazy in love with each other. Still and even more so. There's a reason we haven't been in touch with you, and I'd like to explain. Not so much by way of apology (though partly), but because I think it's kind of interesting.

You know how when you're a kid, you learn that Bambi's father, the Great Stag of the Forest, goes off into the woods to die by himself. When you're in college you learn the same thing, only they call it cultural anthropology. When an old Eskimo lady loses her teeth and can't chew on hide to soften it for clothing, she goes off from the village to die alone in arctic isolation. Nathaniel West used to say that people went toLos Angelesto die in the same kind of way.

Well it's really like that. When I was scheduled to die, Yo Yo and I kind of went off by ourselves; we retreated into psychic isolation. No calls, no dinner invitations, no cocktail parties, no public facade. You retreat from the world, you try to gather yourself together, you pack your gear, and you get ready for transit.

Only I never tripped out. I don't know what happened, and I don't really know what's happening now. I am not cured, I am not in remission, I am not normal, not healthy, not well, but neither am I dying. I am a lot of nots, and no ams. I have a case of terminal limbo. It's a lot of spooky, and I enter hospitals now with the same spookiness that I used to enter movie theaters to see Dracula and Wolfman movies when I was a kid. I knew they weren't for real, but I was nervous and scared anyway.

Lots of things have happened on different levels of our lives. We sold the farm. It was a gorgeous fantasy life that didn't seem to be fun anymore. More than that, we wanted to marshal our assets for the long haul, for estate planning. "Get your papers in order," the doctor had said. That was his euphemism when he first told me I was dying. I hadn't understood. Would you?

My mind just couldn't or wouldn't comprehend his damned delicacy. I thought he wanted me to sign some hospital papers, releases, wavers, something, anything. Huh? I'd said. You know, your papers, he said. What papers, I'd said, and then, slowly dawning over me, I said, you mean my will? And he smiled very gently and benevolently, like James Mason in "Heaven Can Wait," and I'd hated him for his gentility and indirectness and subtlety, and I suppose mostly for his news.

Anyhow, we moved toHouston. Bought a townhouse. Settled down, settled in. Began a new – may I say it? – life. There's no pretty ribbon to wrap it all neatly in, but I've turned Jack Benny's age now – thirty-nine – and at this strange threshold of my life I feel simply happy. There's so much I've done and gone through, and I feel good and proud to have done it, made it, seen it, felt it, and been through it. There's still so much ahead I want to know and touch and feel and understand. I still feel so much potential ahead of me. I want to live so much. Lord, how I'd hate to die now, especially now. Yet – can you understand what I'm driving at? – if I died today, I'd die, not content, but happy.

We are coming out of our shell. We are metamorphosing out of our cocoon. We are rejoining the living. And we extend our hands to you in affection and in hopes of renewing what we view and value as an old, offbeat, and unusual friendship.

Jim

Twenty-eight years have passed and Jim is still with us; alive, successful, and happy. "Life is indeed a crapshoot." For the past fifty years, I have kept a death list of friends and acquaintances. Having a death list sounds morbid, I know, but whenever I add a new name, I glance through the list and am reminded of happy occasions we shared, occasions that have certainly enriched my life. In that way, those on my death list continue to live. And it makes me feel better to know that in the same way I will continue to live in the memories of others after I too am gone.

Sometimes it is hard to understand that people see you differently than you see yourself. I have been receiving compliments for years on how young I look, so you can imagine my surprise when one summer night, about thirty years ago, while Mimi was visiting her mother in Hollywood, I went to the movies. I said, "One, please." The cashier said, "Is that a senior citizen?" I asked her how old that would be, thinking it may be fifty-five years, but she said, "Sixty-five," to which I said, "Yes, please," without further comment. I was already sixty-nine. The passage of my own mortality is written on the aging faces of my friends, and, evidently, on my own face as well.

In the beginning, my life moved very slowly. Then, the older I got the faster it moved, and in recent years my life has actually been racing. The years seem to go by with the speed of months. Under the circumstances, it is to be expected that my mind turns to the subject of dying. Living through the act of dying may be seen as life's ultimate adventure but it may also be seen as the ultimate disappointment that life holds in store, and the one that perhaps tests our mettle to the utmost.

However, it is probably a big mistake to create such a fuss about dying. If you think about it, it's such a commonplace. Everybody does it; Napoleon, Einstein, Stalin, Socrates, Moses, President Roosevelt, Winston Churchill, Clark Gable, Greta Garbo, and Laurence Olivier.

Ever since these various thoughts floated through my mind, dying was no longer the BIG problem. And don't forget, for me at least, there is also the heroin injection that Mimi has been delegated to get me, knowing only too well that it's illegal. That last beautiful orgasm will be buttressed by the serenity and sense of nobility induced with those gratuitous shots of morphine. So, instead of the sadness of helplessly watching someone else die, I will go through the experience of acting it out and actually living through it myself.

In preparation, I have built a granite sarcophagus for two: one side for me, the other side for Mimi. There being no family crest, I had the Custom Shop logo carved into each of the four corners. To complete my preparations, I made a will and wrote my own epitaph, "Levitt was no stuffed shirt."

Keep smiling!

Epilogue

We have just returned from Campbell's Funeral Parlor, January 24, 2003. We were at a private funeral for Al Hirschfeld, the most famous American caricaturist ever and certainly the most talented. Al was to have celebrated his hundredth birthday this coming June. Coincidentally, George Burns also died months before his hundredth birthday.

I have been to endless funerals at Campbell's (it's just around the corner), but this is the first time one couldn't get in without an invitation, and all names were checked in the lobby. The funeral was called for 11:30 and we arrived early at 11:05, and yet there were no seats because the room was full. I got Mimi squeezed into the back row next to friends and I, the aggressive me, took a seat in the second row, in seats reserved for family.

Al's death was totally unexpected because he was so fit. In fact, the day before he died, he put in a full day's work, creating caricatures, once again, of the Marx Brothers. In a prior week, *The New York Times* had published his caricatures for a new Broadway show. Mimi said the speeches were memorable. Unfortunately, I couldn't understand a word because of my impaired hearing, so Louise, Al's wife, will send me copies.

I'm back home now, my agent is coming for lunch and I have been ruminating. Happily, until now, I have not really been moved by death –the deaths of my mother, my father, and those of former friends – each one paying their price for having been born. Oddly enough, or maybe not so odd, Bernbaum's death affected me. So did Fifi's (Manya Starr), and of course, Hirschfeld's. He and Louise were to be guests next week. I knew Al for sixty-one years, having met him through Victor Thall III in 1942.

The next day, Peter Kimmelman telephoned to tell me that Irene Diamond, too, had died in her sleep. Although Irene did have some trouble with her lungs, she was ninety-two, perky, and still very active. Irene was visible at many, many, benefits for organizations who had received some of Irene's largess. She contributed altogether some $500,000,000 divided nicely between the arts and research for AIDS. She supported Dr. Wu and paid for relatively enormous new up-to-date laboratories, which fortunately, created medications that diluted the vicious fatality of AIDS, a disease that is fast becoming a worldwide plague.

I have become accustomed to seeing friends with canes, friends who find it difficult to sit down on a chair and even more difficult to get up. So you might say, at this moment, I am overwhelmed by the proximity of death. It kind of started with David Brockman, Herbert Salzman, Paul Brauer, Ed Ross, and, and … and now I'm drenched.

It's long been a joke in our family, that because my grandfather lived to be ninety-four, it made sense that I could live to one hundred and four, not one hundred and five because that would be greedy. On the other hand, I know that life is a crapshoot, so I cannot look forward to eight more years of being, "fit as a fiddle."

It is better for me to understand that living through the act of dying is indeed life's ultimate adventure, while recognizing that there is no timetable. Am I sad? No. I get up and look forward to my days because I am busy, busy, busy: smiling has become second nature. Although I really am too busy to die, so was Al and so was Irene; so there you are, Keep Smiling.

About the Author: *Mortimer Levitt*

Mortimer Levitt, a high school flunk out, was born in Brooklyn in 1907. He has been successful in business, in the arts, in music, in education, and as a husband. Mortimer and Mimi have been married for fifty-four years and are still going strong. Despite his miserable showing in high school, his major interest now is education and he has created a unique course for Bard College, a unique course for Mercy College, and a unique course for a group of high schools in Lawrence Long Island. All three courses are currently being offered. He is presently at work on his sixth book, proving –if proof were needed– that there is indeed life beyond the age of dying.